ÉDITION FRANÇAISE

ENGLISH
FOR EVERYONE

MANUEL D'APPRENTISSAGE

NIVEAU ❶ DÉBUTANT

L'auteur

Rachel Harding a étudié l'enseignement de la langue anglaise et travaille désormais à plein temps en tant qu'auteur de matériel d'apprentissage de l'anglais. Elle a écrit pour de grands éditeurs de langue anglaise, y compris Oxford University Press.

Les consultants pédagogiques

Tim Bowen a enseigné l'anglais et formé des enseignants dans plus de trente pays. Il est le coauteur d'ouvrages sur l'enseignement de la prononciation et sur la méthodologie de l'enseignement des langues, et est l'auteur de nombreux ouvrages pour les enseignants d'anglais. Il travaille actuellement comme auteur indépendant de matériels pédagogique, éditeur et traducteur. Il est membre du Chartered Institute of Linguists.

Kate O'Donovan, irlandaise, est titulaire d'un PDGE, et d'une licence d'histoire et d'anglais. Elle a travaillé en Suisse, à Oman et au Bahreïn. Depuis 2014 à Paris, elle enseigne l'anglais au British Council où elle est aussi coordinatrice.

La consultante linguistique

Susan Barduhn est professeur d'anglais et formatrice expérimentée d'enseignants. Elle a, en tant qu'auteur, contribué à de nombreuses publications. Elle donne non seulement des cours d'anglais dans le monde entier, mais est également présidente de l'Association internationale des professeurs d'anglais langue étrangère et conseillère auprès du Conseil britannique et du département d'État américain. Elle est actuellement professeur à la School for International Training dans le Vermont, aux États-Unis.

ÉDITION FRANÇAISE

ENGLISH
FOR EVERYONE

MANUEL D'APPRENTISSAGE
NIVEAU 1 DÉBUTANT

Aa

DK

Rédacteurs Gareth Clark, Lisa Gillepsie, Andrew Kerr-Jarrett
Éditeurs artistiques Chrissy Barnard, Ray Bryant
Éditeur artistique senior Sharon Spencer
Assistants d'édition Jessica Cawthra, Sarah Edwards
Illustrateurs Edwood Burn, Denise Joos,
Michael Parkin, Jemma Westing
Producteur audio Liz Hammond
Rédacteur en chef Daniel Mills
Éditeur artistique en chef Anna Hall
Gestionnaire de projet Christine Stroyan
Concepteur couverture Natalie Godwin
Éditeur couverture Claire Gellw
Responsable conception couverture Sophia MTT
Production, préproduction Luca Frassinetti
Production Mary Slater
Éditeur Andrew Macintyre
Directeur artistique Karen Self
Directeur de publication Jonathan Metcalf

DK Inde
Concepteur couverture Surabhi Wadhwa
Éditeur couvertures en chef Saloni Singh
Concepteur PAO en chef Harish Aggarwal

Publié en Grande-Bretagne en 2016
par Dorling Kindersley Limited
DK, One Embassy Gardens,
8 Viaduct Gardens, London, SW11 7BW

Le représentant autorisé dans l'EEE est
Dorling Kindersley Verlag GmbH. Arnulfstra. 124,
80636 Munich, Allemagne

Titre original : *English For Everyone. Course Book.
Level 1. Beginner*

Adaptation et réalisation : Édiclic
Révision pédagogique : Kate O'Donovan
Traduction : Estelle Demontrond-Box pour Édiclic
Lecture-correction : Paul Cléonie

ISBN : 978-0-2413-0242-2
Imprimé et relié en Slovaquie

Pour les esprits curieux
www.dk.com

Sommaire

Fonctionnement du cours

English for everyone est un ouvrage conçu pour toutes les personnes désireuses d'apprendre l'anglais par elles-mêmes. Comme tout cours de langue, il porte sur les compétences de base : grammaire, vocabulaire, prononciation, compréhension orale, expression orale, compréhension écrite et expression écrite. Ici, les compétences sont enseignées de façon visuelle, à l'aide d'images et de schémas pour vous aider à comprendre et à bien mémoriser. Pour être plus efficace, suivez la progression du livre en veillant à utiliser les enregistrements à votre disposition sur le site Internet et sur l'application. À la fin de chaque unité, vous pouvez effectuer les exercices supplémentaires dans le livre d'exercices afin de renforcer votre apprentissage.

LIVRE D'EXERCICES

MANUEL D'APPRENTISSAGE

Numéro de chapitre Il vous aide à suivre votre progression.

Les points d'apprentissage Chaque chapitre débute par un résumé des points d'apprentissage clés.

Modules Chaque chapitre est divisé en modules, qui doivent être réalisés dans l'ordre. Vous pouvez faire une pause à la fin de chaque module.

Apprentissage linguistique Les modules avec un fond coloré vous enseignent un nouveau vocabulaire et une nouvelle grammaire. Étudiez-les attentivement avant de faire les exercices.

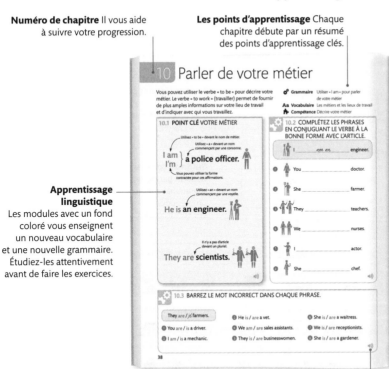

Support audio La plupart des modules sont accompagnés d'enregistrements sonores de locuteurs anglophones pour vous aider à améliorer vos compétences en matière de compréhension et d'expression orales.

Exercices Les modules sur fond blanc vous proposent des exercices destinés à renforcer vos connaissances.

AUDIO GRATUIT
Site Internet et appli
www.dkefe.com

Modules linguistiques

Les nouveaux points sont enseignés de manière progressive : d'abord une explication simple de leur emploi, puis des exemples supplémentaires de leur emploi courant et une explication détaillée de leurs constructions clés.

Numéro de module Chaque module est identifié par un numéro unique qui vous permet d'évaluer votre progression et de trouver facilement les enregistrements associés.

Titre de module Le point enseigné apparaît ici avec une introduction courte.

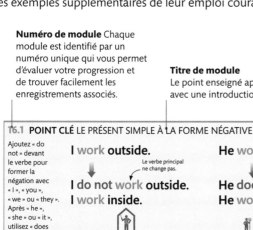

16.1 POINT CLÉ LE PRÉSENT SIMPLE À LA FORME NÉGATIVE

Ajoutez « do not » devant le verbe pour former la négation avec « I », « you », « we » ou « they ». Après « he », « she » ou « it », utilisez « does not ».

I **work** outside.

Le verbe principal ne change pas.

I do not **work** outside.
I **work** inside.

He **works** inside.

He does not **work** inside.
He **works** outside.

Exemples linguistiques Les exemples sont contextualisés. La couleur permet de repérer facilement les nouvelles constructions expliquées par des annotations.

Guide graphique Des images ou pictogrammes clairs et simples facilitent également l'apprentissage et la mémorisation.

16.2 AUTRES EXEMPLES LE PRÉSENT SIMPLE À LA FORME NÉGATIVE

You do not **have** a laptop.

We do not **start** work at 8am.

He does not **live** in Los Angeles.

The house does not **have** a backyard.

Enregistrements associés Ce symbole indique que les phrases modèles sont disponibles en enregistrements audio.

16.3 CONSTRUCTION LE PRÉSENT SIMPLE À LA FORME NÉGATIVE

Utilisez « do » ou « does » avec « not » suivi du radical (infinitif sans « to ») du verbe principal.

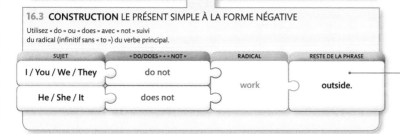

SUJET	« DO/DOES » + « NOT »	RADICAL	RESTE DE LA PHRASE
I / You / We / They	do not	work	outside.
He / She / It	does not		

Guide de construction Ces aides visuelles permettent de décomposer la grammaire anglaise en éléments simples pour repérer et recréer des constructions, même complexes.

Vocabulaire Tout au long du manuel, vous trouverez des modules de vocabulaire avec des expressions et mots anglais courants et utiles, accompagnés d'images pour vous aider à les mémoriser.

Espace pour écrire Il est recommandé que vous écriviez vous-même les traductions pour conserver une trace à titre de référence.

Modules d'exercices

Chaque exercice est soigneusement conçu pour mettre en pratique et tester les nouveaux points linguistiques enseignés dans les chapitres correspondants du manuel d'apprentissage. Les exercices accompagnant le manuel vous aideront à mieux mémoriser ce que vous avez appris et donc à mieux maîtriser la langue anglaise. Chaque exercice est introduit par un symbole indiquant la compétence travaillée.

 GRAMMAIRE
Appliquez les règles grammaticales dans des contextes différents.

 COMPRÉHENSION ÉCRITE
Étudiez la langue dans des contextes anglophones authentiques.

 COMPRÉHENSION ORALE
Évaluez votre niveau de compréhension de l'anglais oral.

 VOCABULAIRE
Consolidez votre compréhension du vocabulaire clé.

 EXPRESSION ORALE
Comparez votre anglais oral aux enregistrements audio types.

Numéro de module
Chaque module est identifié par un numéro unique qui vous permet de trouver facilement les réponses et les enregistrements associés.

Consignes des exercices Chaque exercice est introduit par une consigne courte qui vous explique ce que vous devez faire.

Exemple de réponse La réponse des premières questions de chaque exercice vous est donnée pour vous aider à mieux comprendre la consigne.

Espace pour écrire
Il est recommandé que vous écriviez vos réponses dans le livre pour garder une trace et évaluer vos résultats.

13.10 COMPLÉTEZ LES PHRASES EN CONJUGUANT CORRECTEMENT LES VERBES.

He _finishes_ (finish) work at 5 o'clock.

1. Lucia _____ (wake) up at 7am.
2. I _____ (get) up at 7:30am.
3. Ethan _____ (go) to work at 5am.
4. You _____ (leave) work at 5pm.
5. Shona _____ (watch) TV in the evening.

Supports graphiques
Des images ou pictogrammes sont fournis afin de vous aider à comprendre les exercices.

Supports audio Ce symbole indique que les réponses de l'exercice sont disponibles sous forme d'enregistrements audio. Écoutez-les une fois l'exercice terminé.

29.11 COMPLÉTEZ LES PHRASES, PUIS LISEZ-LES À VOIX HAUTE.

Has Milo got a washing machine?
No, _he hasn't_ .

1. Has she got a toaster?
Yes, _____ .
2. Has the house got a dining room?
Yes, _____ .
3. Have they got a new refrigerator?
No, _____ .
4. Has it got a large kitchen?
No, _____ .

Exercice de compréhension orale
Ce symbole indique que vous devez écouter un enregistrement audio afin de répondre aux questions de l'exercice.

Exercice d'expression orale
Ce symbole indique que vous devez donner les réponses à voix haute, puis que vous devez les comparer aux enregistrements types compris dans les fichiers audio.

45.12 BON OU PAS ? ÉCOUTEZ, PUIS COCHEZ LA BONNE RÉPONSE.

Good at ☑ Bad at ☐
1. Good at ☐ Bad at ☐
2. Good at ☐ Bad at ☐
3. Good at ☐ Bad at ☐
4. Good at ☐ Bad at ☐

Audio

English for everyone contient de nombreux documents audio. Il vous est recommandé de les utiliser autant que possible, afin d'améliorer votre compréhension de l'anglais parlé et d'avoir un accent et une prononciation plus naturels. Chaque dossier peut être lu, mis en pause ou répété aussi souvent que vous le désirez, jusqu'à ce que vous soyez sûr d'avoir parfaitement compris ce qui a été dit.

EXERCICES DE COMPRÉHENSION ORALE
Ce symbole indique que vous devez écouter un enregistrement afin de pouvoir répondre aux questions d'un exercice.

AUDIO ASSOCIÉ
Ce symbole indique qu'un enregistrement supplémentaire est à votre disposition une fois le module terminé.

AUDIO GRATUIT
Site Internet et appli
www.dkefe.com

Suivez votre progression

La méthode est conçue pour vous permettre de suivre votre progression grâce à des modules d'analyses et des récapitulatifs réguliers. Les réponses aux exercices sont fournies et vous pouvez ainsi vérifier votre compréhension de chaque élément pédagogique.

Check-lists Chaque chapitre se termine par une check-list afin de vérifier les nouvelles compétences apprises.

Modules bilan À la fin de chaque unité, vous trouverez un module bilan plus détaillé résumant les points linguistiques appris.

Cases à cocher Utilisez ces cases pour indiquer les compétences que vous pensez avoir assimilées. Revenez en arrière et retravaillez tout point que vous pensez ne pas encore maîtriser.

Réponses Trouvez les réponses de chaque exercice à la fin du manuel.

Numéros des exercices Faites-les correspondre avec l'identifiant unique situé au coin supérieur gauche de chaque exercice.

Audio Ce symbole indique qu'il vous est possible d'écouter les réponses.

01 Vous présenter

Vous pouvez saluer d'autres personnes en disant « Hello! » ou « Hi! ». Pour vous présenter, dites « I am ». Vous aurez peut-être également besoin d'épeler votre nom.

⚙ **Grammaire** « To be » pour dire votre nom

Aa Vocabulaire Dire votre nom et les lettres de l'alphabet

🧩 **Compétence** Dire comment vous vous appelez

1.1 POINT CLÉ DIRE VOTRE NOM

Vous pouvez saluer quelqu'un et vous présenter de différentes façons.

Cette salutation peut être formelle ou informelle.

Hello! I am Lyla.

Pour vous présenter, vous pouvez utiliser « I am » suivi de votre nom.

Ceci est une salutation informelle. Elle est souvent utilisée lors de conversations courantes.

Hi! My name is Joe.

Pour vous présenter, vous pouvez aussi utiliser « My name is » suivi de votre nom.

1.2 AUTRES EXEMPLES DIRE VOTRE NOM

En anglais parlé, les locuteurs utilisent souvent les contractions. Une contraction est la version abrégée de deux mots.

I am Lyla.

⬇

I'm Lyla.

Vous pouvez utiliser la forme contractée « I'm » au lieu de « I am ».

My name is Joe.

⬇

My name's Joe.

Vous pouvez utiliser la forme contractée « name's » au lieu de « name is ».

1.3 CONSTRUCTION DIRE VOTRE NOM

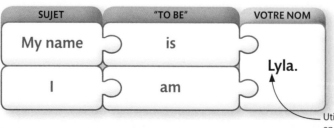

SUJET	"TO BE"	VOTRE NOM
My name	is	
I	am	Lyla.

Utilisez une lettre majuscule en début de nom.

1.4 RÉCRIVEZ LES PHRASES À LA FORME CONTRACTÉE.

> My name is Jack.
> *My name's Jack.*

1 I am Charlotte.

_____

2 My name is Una.

_____

3 My name is Simone.

_____

4 I am Carlos.

_____

5 I am Juan.

_____

6 My name is Miriam.

_____

7 I am Sarah.

_____

🔊

1.5 ÉCOUTEZ L'ENREGISTREMENT, PUIS NUMÉROTEZ LES PERSONNAGES DANS LE BON ORDRE.

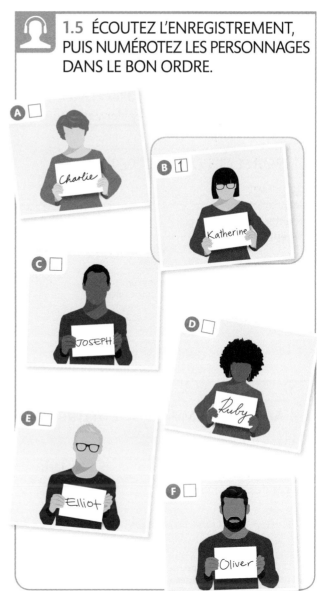

1.6 UTILISEZ LE SCHÉMA POUR CRÉER 12 PHRASES CORRECTES, PUIS LISEZ-LES À VOIX HAUTE.

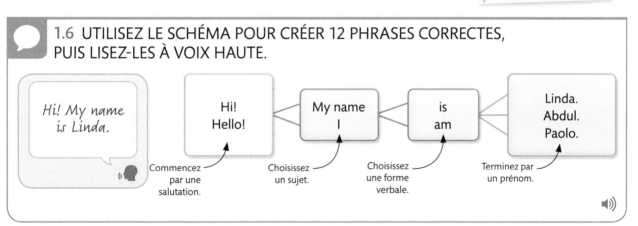

Hi! My name is Linda.

| Hi! Hello! | My name / I | is / am | Linda. Abdul. Paolo. |

Commencez par une salutation.

Choisissez un sujet.

Choisissez une forme verbale.

Terminez par un prénom.

🔊

13

1.7 **POINT CLÉ** ÉPELER VOTRE NOM

How do you spell your first name?

Voici la façon dont on demande à quelqu'un d'épeler son prénom.

My name's Jacob, J-A-C-O-B.

Vous prononcez chaque lettre.

How do you spell your last name?

Voici la façon dont on demande à quelqu'un d'épeler son nom de famille.

Williams, W-I-L-L-I-A-M-S.

How do you spell your full name?

On vous demande votre prénom et votre nom de famille.

J-A-C-O-B W-I-L-L-I-A-M-S.

1.8 **PRONONCIATION** L'ALPHABET

Écoutez la prononciation des lettres de l'alphabet en anglais.

Aa Bb Cc Dd Ee Ff Gg Hh Ii

Jj Kk Ll Mm Nn Oo Pp Qq

Rr Ss Tt Uu Vv Ww Xx Yy Zz

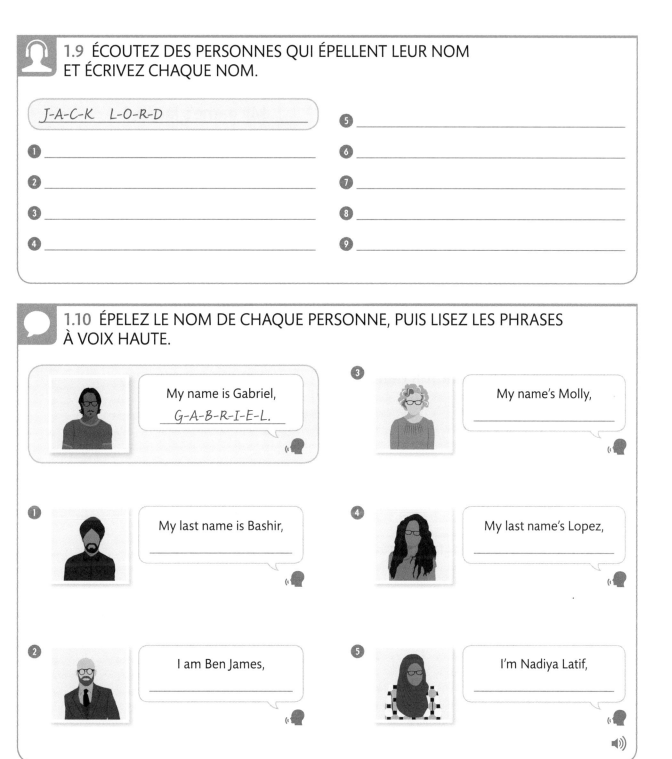

1.9 ÉCOUTEZ DES PERSONNES QUI ÉPELLENT LEUR NOM ET ÉCRIVEZ CHAQUE NOM.

J-A-C-K L-O-R-D

1 _____

2 _____

3 _____

4 _____

5 _____

6 _____

7 _____

8 _____

9 _____

1.10 ÉPELEZ LE NOM DE CHAQUE PERSONNE, PUIS LISEZ LES PHRASES À VOIX HAUTE.

My name is Gabriel,
G-A-B-R-I-E-L.

3 My name's Molly,
_____

1 My last name is Bashir,
_____

4 My last name's Lopez,
_____

2 I am Ben James,
_____

5 I'm Nadiya Latif,
_____

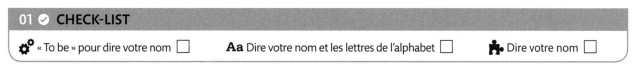

01 ✓ CHECK-LIST

⚙ « To be » pour dire votre nom ☐   **Aa** Dire votre nom et les lettres de l'alphabet ☐   🧩 Dire votre nom ☐

2.1 LES PAYS

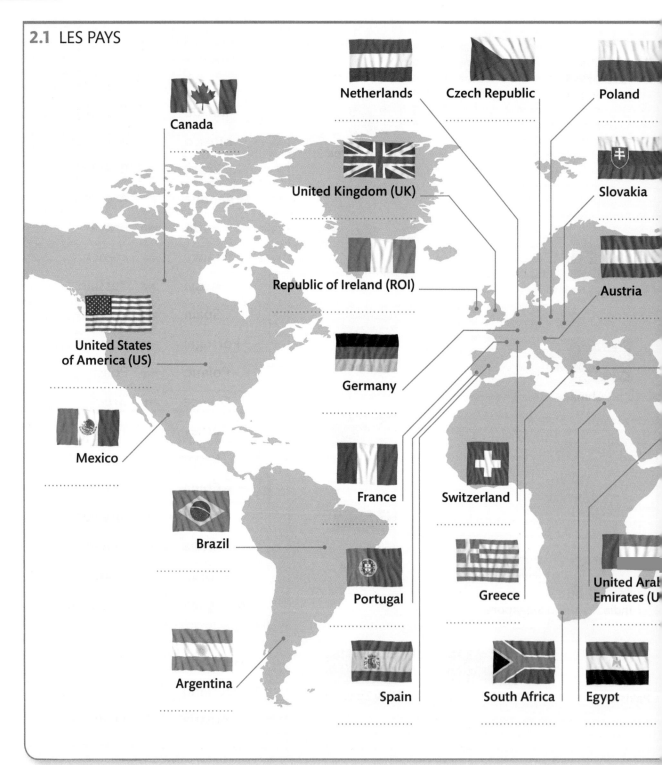

Netherlands

Czech Republic

Poland

Canada

United Kingdom (UK)

Slovakia

Republic of Ireland (ROI)

Austria

United States
of America (US)

Germany

Mexico

France   Switzerland

Brazil

Portugal   Greece   United Arab
Emirates (U

Argentina

Spain   South Africa   Egypt

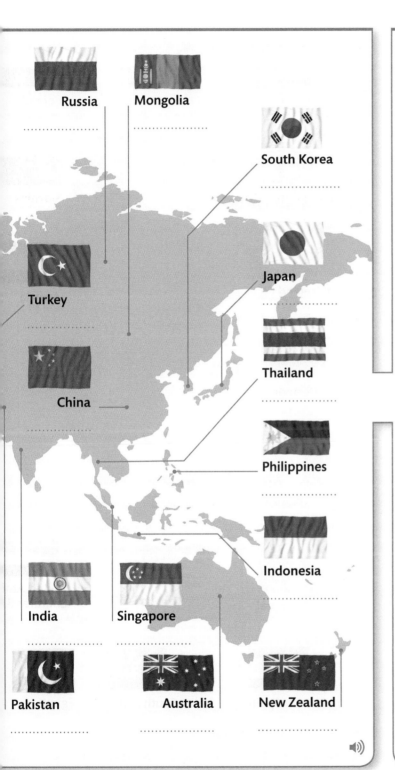

Russia

Mongolia

South Korea

Japan

Turkey

Thailand

China

Philippines

India Singapore

Indonesia

Pakistan Australia New Zealand

🔊

2.2 NATIONALITÉS

USA	➡	American
Canada	➡	Canadian
Mexico	➡	Mexican
Brazil	➡	Brazilian
Argentina	➡	Argentinian
UK	➡	British
France	➡	French
Russia	➡	Russian
Spain	➡	Spanish
Portugal	➡	Portuguese
Poland	➡	Polish
Greece	➡	Greek
Turkey	➡	Turkish
Egypt	➡	Egyptian
China	➡	Chinese
Japan	➡	Japanese
India	➡	Indian
Pakistan	➡	Pakistani
Mongolia	➡	Mongolian
Australia	➡	Australian
Germany	➡	German
Switzerland	➡	Swiss
Austria	➡	Austrian

🔊

Il est utile de savoir comment dire son âge et d'où l'on vient. Pour cela, vous pouvez utiliser le verbe « to be ».

⚙ **Grammaire** « To be » avec l'âge et la nationalité

Aa Vocabulaire Les nombres et les nationalités

🧩 **Compétence** Parler de vous

3.1 **POINT CLÉ** DIRE VOTRE ÂGE

Utilisez le verbe « to be » pour dire votre âge.

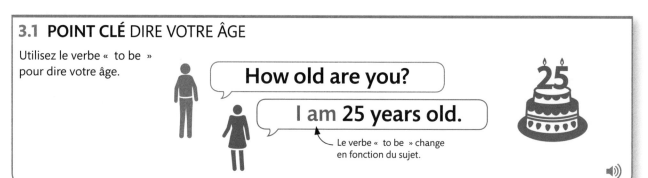

How old are you?

I am **25 years old.**

Le verbe « to be » change en fonction du sujet.

🔊

3.2 **AUTRES EXEMPLES** DIRE VOTRE ÂGE

Ruby is **seven years old.**

I'm **44 today.**

Izzy and Chloe are **13.**

My grandma is **92 years old.**

🔊

3.3 **CONSTRUCTION** DIRE VOTRE ÂGE

SUJET	« TO BE »	VOTRE ÂGE
I	am	
You	are	**25 years old.**
He / She / It	is	
We / They	are	

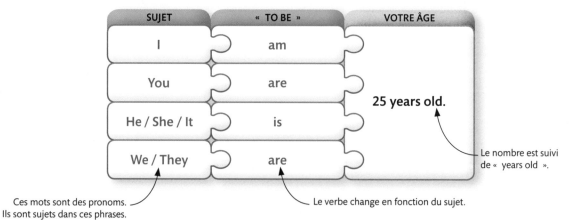

Le nombre est suivi de « years old ».

Ces mots sont des pronoms. Ils sont sujets dans ces phrases.

Le verbe change en fonction du sujet.

3.4 **VOCABULAIRE** LES NOMBRES

1 one	2 two	3 three	4 four	5 five	6 six
7 seven	8 eight	9 nine	10 ten	11 eleven	12 twelve
13 thirteen	14 fourteen	15 fifteen	16 sixteen	17 seventeen	18 eighteen
19 nineteen	20 twenty	21 twenty-one	22 twenty-two	30 thirty	40 forty
50 fifty	60 sixty	70 seventy	80 eighty	90 ninety	100 one hundred

🔊

Aa 3.5 ÉCRIVEZ LES NOMBRES EN TOUTES LETTRES.

3 = _____*three*_____

1. 11 = _____
2. 17 = _____
3. 34 = _____
4. 59 = _____
5. 85 = _____

🔊

3.6 COMPLÉTEZ EN CONJUGUANT « TO BE » À LA BONNE FORME.

Michael _____*is*_____ 32 years old.

1. Theo _____ 45 years old.
2. Madison _____ 27 years old.
3. Jeremy and Tanya _____ 90 years old.
4. We _____ 29 years old.
5. I _____ 34 years old.

🔊

3.7 PRONONCIATION LES NOMBRES À CONSONANCE SIMILAIRE

Il est important de marquer l'accent tonique sur les bonnes syllabes dans les nombres suivants :

Accentuez la dernière syllabe. / Accentuez la première syllabe.

13	**Thirteen**	30	**Thirty**
14	**Fourteen**	40	**Forty**
15	**Fifteen**	50	**Fifty**
16	**Sixteen**	60	**Sixty**
17	**Seventeen**	70	**Seventy**
18	**Eighteen**	80	**Eighty**
19	**Nineteen**	90	**Ninety**

3.8 ÉCOUTEZ L'ENREGISTREMENT ET COCHEZ L'ÂGE CORRECT.

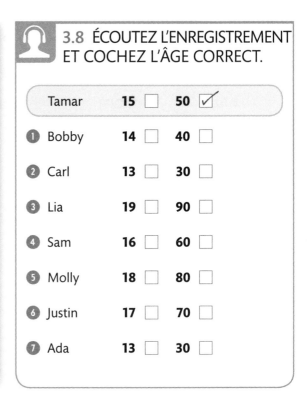

Tamar	**15** ☐	**50** ☑
❶ Bobby	**14** ☐	**40** ☐
❷ Carl	**13** ☐	**30** ☐
❸ Lia	**19** ☐	**90** ☐
❹ Sam	**16** ☐	**60** ☐
❺ Molly	**18** ☐	**80** ☐
❻ Justin	**17** ☐	**70** ☐
❼ Ada	**13** ☐	**30** ☐

3.9 POINT CLÉ DIRE D'OÙ VOUS VENEZ

Vous pouvez dire d'où vous venez de différentes façons.

« Where » est le mot interrogatif pour le lieu.

Where are you from?

N'oubliez pas que la conjugaison de « to be » change en fonction du sujet.

I am from Spain.

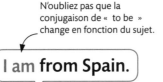

Ceci décrit le pays auquel vous appartenez.

What nationality are you?

Vous utilisez un adjectif pour indiquer votre nationalité.

I'm Spanish.

3.10 AUTRES EXEMPLES DIRE D'OÙ VOUS VENEZ

I am Dutch.

We are Italian.

I'm from Switzerland.

20

3.11 CONSTRUCTION DIRE D'OÙ VOUS VENEZ

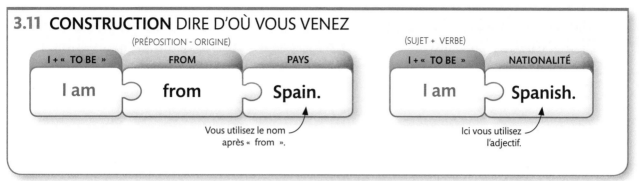

(PRÉPOSITION - ORIGINE)

I + « TO BE »	FROM	PAYS
I am	from	Spain.

Vous utilisez le nom après « from ».

(SUJET + VERBE)

I + « TO BE »	NATIONALITÉ
I am	Spanish.

Ici vous utilisez l'adjectif.

Aa 3.12 RELIEZ CHAQUE DRAPEAU À SON PAYS.

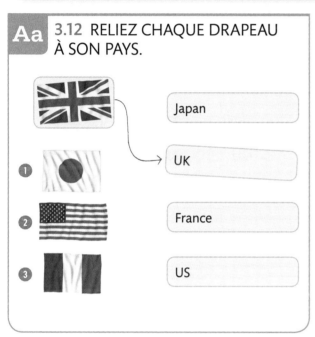

Japan

UK

France

US

3.13 ÉCRIVEZ LA NATIONALITÉ CORRESPONDANT À CHAQUE PAYS.

Italy	=	*Italian*
❶ Spain	=	_____
❷ Germany	=	_____
❸ Canada	=	_____
❹ America	=	_____
❺ Australia	=	_____
❻ China	=	_____

◀))

3.14 UTILISEZ LE SCHÉMA POUR CRÉER 12 PHRASES, PUIS LISEZ-LES À VOIX HAUTE.

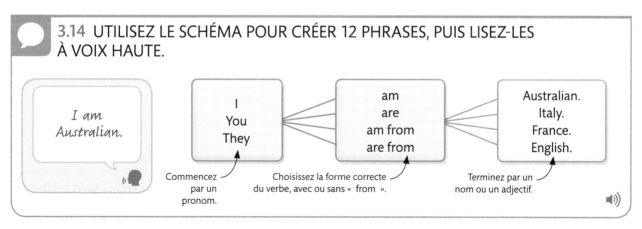

I am Australian.

| I / You / They | am / are / am from / are from | Australian. / Italy. / France. / English. |

Commencez par un pronom.

Choisissez la forme correcte du verbe, avec ou sans « from ».

Terminez par un nom ou un adjectif.

◀))

---

04 Vocabulaire

4.1 LA FAMILLE DE PABLO

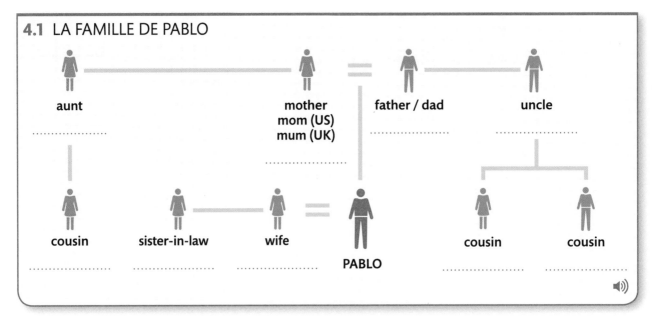

aunt

mother
mom (US)
mum (UK)

father / dad

uncle

cousin

sister-in-law

wife

PABLO

cousin

cousin

4.2 LA FAMILLE DE MARY

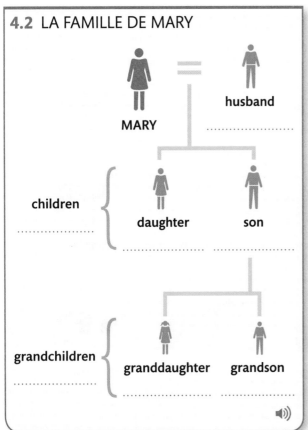

husband

MARY

children

daughter

son

grandchildren

granddaughter

grandson

4.3 LA FAMILLE DE SARAH

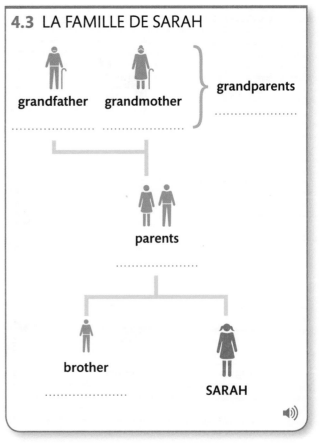

grandfather

grandmother

grandparents

parents

brother

SARAH

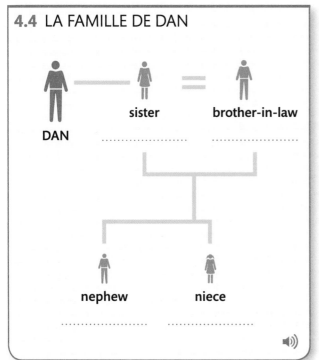

4.4 LA FAMILLE DE DAN

DAN

sister = brother-in-law

nephew

niece

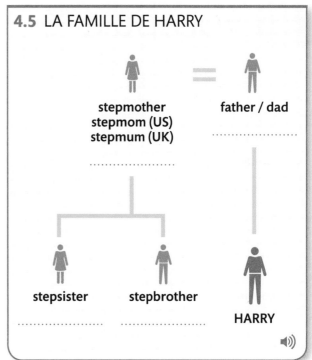

4.5 LA FAMILLE DE HARRY

stepmother
stepmom (US)
stepmum (UK)

father / dad

stepsister

stepbrother

HARRY

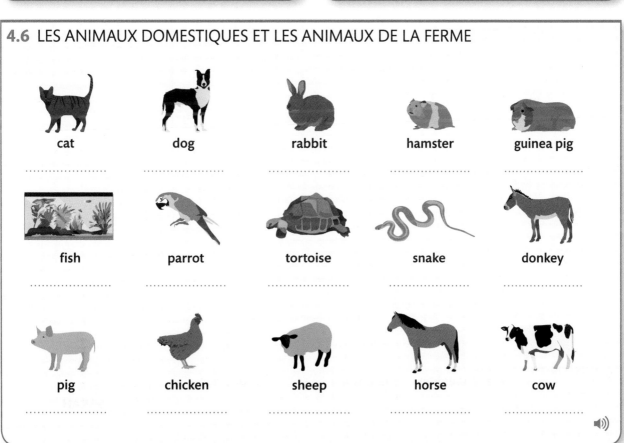

4.6 LES ANIMAUX DOMESTIQUES ET LES ANIMAUX DE LA FERME

cat

dog

rabbit

hamster

guinea pig

fish

parrot

tortoise

snake

donkey

pig

chicken

sheep

horse

cow

05 Exprimer la possession

Les adjectifs possessifs permettent d'indiquer à qui quelque chose appartient (un animal domestique, par exemple). « This » et « that » sont des déterminants. Ils mettent l'accent sur un objet ou une personne spécifique.

⚙ **Grammaire** Les adjectifs possessifs, « this » et « that »
Aa Vocabulaire Les animaux et la famille
🧩 **Compétence** Dire à qui quelque chose appartient

5.1 POINT CLÉ LES ADJECTIFS POSSESSIFS

Les adjectifs possessifs se placent devant le nom.
Ils se modifient selon que le propriétaire est singulier, pluriel, masculin ou féminin, la personne à qui vous parlez ou vous-même.

Felix is my cat.

Le chat m'appartient.

Coco is your rabbit.

Le lapin vous appartient (ou t'appartient).

Buster is her dog.

Le chien lui appartient (à elle).

Polly is his parrot.

Le perroquet lui appartient (à lui).

Rachel is our daughter.

Elle est notre fille.

John is their son.

Il est leur fils.

🔊

5.2 CONSTRUCTION LES ADJECTIFS POSSESSIFS

I	you	he	she	it	we	they
⬇	⬇	⬇	⬇	⬇	⬇	⬇
my	your	his	her	its	our	their
⬇	⬇	⬇	⬇	⬇	⬇	⬇
my cat	your rabbit	his wife	her sister	its ball	our horse	their son

🔊

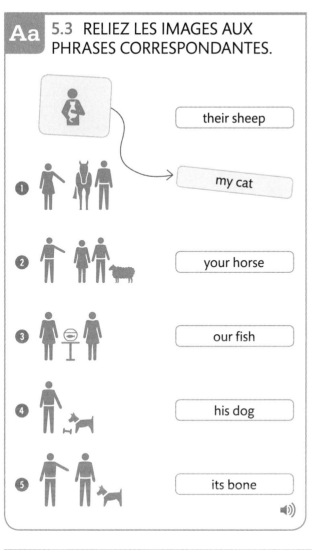

Aa 5.3 RELIEZ LES IMAGES AUX PHRASES CORRESPONDANTES.

- ❶ their sheep
- → my cat
- ❷ your horse
- ❸ our fish
- ❹ his dog
- ❺ its bone

5.4 COMPLÉTEZ LES PHRASES AVEC LES ADJECTIFS POSSESSIFS CORRECTS.

_____Her_____ (She) name is Mary.

❶ Bingo is _____ (I) dog.

❷ _____ (She) aunt is called Goldie.

❸ _____ (I) cat eats fish.

❹ _____ (They) rabbit lives in the backyard.

❺ _____ (We) parrot is from Colombia.

❻ _____ (He) wife is called Henrietta.

❼ _____ (They) dog is 10 years old.

❽ _____ (We) aunt lives on a farm in Ohio.

❾ Here is _____ (it) ball.

5.5 RÉCRIVEZ LES PHRASES SUIVANTES EN CORRIGEANT LES ERREURS.

Nick are my brother.
Nick is my brother.

❶ Farida are their sister.
_____

❷ Duke am our dog.
_____

❸ Daisy are her mother.
_____

❹ They is his grandparents.
_____

❺ It am our horse.
_____

❻ John am our cousin.
_____

❼ I are Daisy's daughter.
_____

❽ You is my friend.
_____

5.6 POINT CLÉ « THIS » ET « THAT »

« This » et « that » sont des déterminants. Ils mettent l'accent sur un objet ou une personne spécifique dont vous voulez parler. Utilisez « this » pour quelqu'un ou quelque chose qui se trouve près de vous.
Utilisez « that » pour quelqu'un ou quelque chose qui se trouve loin de vous.

This is my dog.

Le chien est près de vous.

That is my dog.

Le chien est loin de vous.

5.7 AUTRES EXEMPLES « THIS » ET « THAT »

This is your rabbit.

That is your rabbit.

This is her horse.

That is her horse.

This is its bed.

That is its bed.

5.8 COMPLÉTEZ LES PHRASES AVEC « THIS » OU « THAT ».

 ___*That*___ is my dog.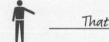

3 _____ is their pig.

1 _____ is her horse.

4 _____ is his cow.

2 _____ is our rabbit.

5 _____ is your fish.

5.9 ÉCRIVEZ LES MOTS SUIVANTS DANS LE BON ORDRE AFIN DE RECONSTITUER LES PHRASES.

| is | horse. | This | his |

This is his horse.

❶ | their | Lily | is | sister. |

_____

❷ | son | old. | 12 | is | years | Our |

_____

❸ | cow. | their | is | That |

_____

❹ | is | ball. | your | This |

_____

❺ | called | Her | Caspar. | father | is |

_____

5.10 ÉCOUTEZ L'ENREGISTREMENT, PUIS NUMÉROTEZ LES IMAGES DANS LE BON ORDRE.

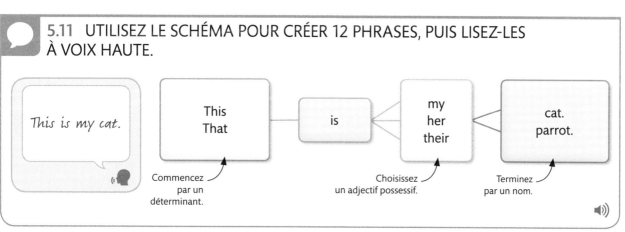

Ⓐ ☐ Ⓑ 1 Ⓒ ☐ Ⓓ ☐ Ⓔ ☐

5.11 UTILISEZ LE SCHÉMA POUR CRÉER 12 PHRASES, PUIS LISEZ-LES À VOIX HAUTE.

This is my cat.

| This / That | is | my / her / their | cat. / parrot. |

Commencez par un déterminant.

Choisissez un adjectif possessif.

Terminez par un nom.

05 ✓ CHECK-LIST

⚙ Les adjectifs possessifs : « this » et « that » ☐ **Aa** Les animaux et la famille ☐ 🧩 Dire à qui quelque chose appartient ☐

06 Utiliser l'apostrophe

En anglais, vous pouvez utiliser l'apostrophe (') pour indiquer la possession. Vous pouvez l'utiliser pour montrer à qui quelque chose appartient (un animal domestique, par exemple) et pour parler de votre famille.

🔧 **Grammaire** L'apostrophe possessive
Aa Vocabulaire La famille et les animaux domestiques
🧩 **Compétence** Parler de ce qui vous appartient

6.1 POINT CLÉ L'APOSTROPHE AVEC « S »

Ajoutez une apostrophe et la lettre « s » à la fin d'un nom singulier pour montrer que ce qui vient après le nom lui appartient.

Cette forme est correcte en anglais mais n'est pas habituellement utilisée.

the mother of Lizzie

⬇

Lizzie's mother

Ceci est la manière la plus usuelle d'exprimer la possession.

Une apostrophe avec un « s » indique la possession.

🔊

6.2 AUTRES EXEMPLES L'APOSTROPHE AVEC « S »

Dave's grandmother

The dog's ball

Tess's dog

On peut aussi écrire Tess'.

Juan and Beth's parrot

Si quelque chose appartient à plus d'un nom, n'ajoutez le « s » qu'à la fin du dernier nom.

🔊

6.3 RÉCRIVEZ LA PHRASE EN UTILISANT UNE APOSTROPHE PLUS « S ».

| The daughter of Kevin | = | *Kevin's daughter* |

❶ The son of Ben = _____

❷ The cat of Sam and Ayshah = _____

❸ The house of Debbie = _____

❹ The car of Marco and Kate = _____

❺ The grandchild of Elsa = _____

❻ The parrot of Beth = _____

🔊

6.4 ÉCOUTEZ ET RELIEZ LES PAIRES.

Edith is → Ben's mother.

❶ Lucas is → Ben's grandmother.

❷ Lily is → Ben's son.

❸ Noah is → Ben's sister.

❹ Grace is → Ben's brother.

❺ Alex is → Ben's father.

6.5 POINT CLÉ L'APOSTROPHE ET LES NOMS PLURIELS

Pour indiquer l'appartenance avec un nom pluriel, ajoutez une apostrophe sans le « s ».

Ginger is my parents' cat.

On utilise une apostrophe sans « s » avec les noms au pluriel.

6.6 AUTRES EXEMPLES L'APOSTROPHE ET LES NOMS PLURIELS

This is my cousins' rabbit.

That is his grandparents' house.

Rex is her brothers' dog.

Polly is our children's parrot.

Pour les noms pluriels qui se terminent sans « s » (forme du pluriel), vous devez ajouter un « -s » (forme de possession).

6.7 ÉCRIVEZ LES MOTS DANS LE BON ORDRE AFIN DE RECONSTITUER LES PHRASES.

| uncle. | Kevin | Sharon's | is |

Kevin is Sharon's uncle.

❶ | Skanda's | is | wife. | Angela |

_____

❷ | snake. | is | my cousins' | That |

_____

❸ | Sue | aunt. | Ella and Mark's | is |

_____

❹ | is | John's | cat. | Ginger |

_____

6.8 COMPLÉTEZ LES PHRASES, PUIS LISEZ-LES À VOIX HAUTE.

Edith is ___Ben's___ (Ben) grandmother.

❶ Kathy is _____ (Dave) aunt.

❷ Rex is _____ (Noah and Pat) dog.

❸ This is _____ (her cousins) house.

❹ Felix is _____ (the children) cat.

06 ✓ CHECK-LIST

⚙ L'apostrophe possessive ☐   **Aa** La famille et les animaux domestiques ☐   🧩 Parler de ce qui vous appartient ☐

Vocabulaire

7.1 LES OBJETS DU QUOTIDIEN

wallet (US)
purse (UK)

wallet

coins

keys

bottle of water

apple

sandwich

cell phone (US)
mobile phone (UK)

camera

earphones

tablet

laptop

pencil

pen

notebook

letter

newspaper

magazine

book / novel

dictionary

map

mirror

toothbrush

umbrella

hairbrush

planner (US)
diary (UK)

glasses

sunglasses

necklace

watch

passport

ID card

Parler de ce qui vous appartient

On utilise « these » et « those » lorsque l'on parle de plusieurs choses. Pour indiquer à qui quelque chose appartient, vous pouvez utiliser des déterminants ou des pronoms possessifs.

⚙ **Grammaire** « These » et « those »
Aa Vocabulaire Vos affaires personnelles
🧩 **Compétence** Les déterminants et les pronoms

8.1 POINT CLÉ « THESE » ET « THOSE »

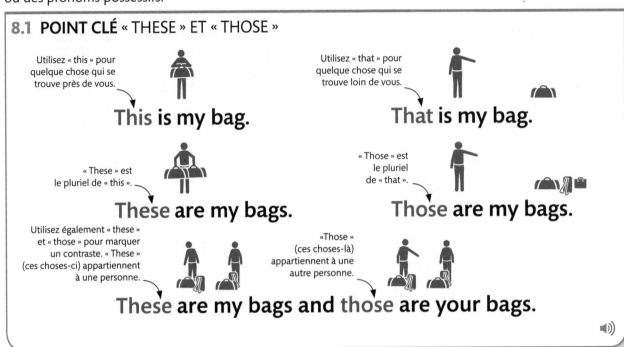

Utilisez « this » pour quelque chose qui se trouve près de vous.

This is my bag.

Utilisez « that » pour quelque chose qui se trouve loin de vous.

That is my bag.

« These » est le pluriel de « this ».

These are my bags.

« Those » est le pluriel de « that ».

Those are my bags.

Utilisez également « these » et « those » pour marquer un contraste. « These » (ces choses-ci) appartiennent à une personne.

«Those» (ces choses-là) appartiennent à une autre personne.

These are my bags and those are your bags.

8.2 BARREZ LE MOT INCORRECT DANS CHAQUE PHRASE.

This / ~~These~~ is my bag.

1 This / These are Diego's keys.

2 This / These is Olivia's purse.

3 That / Those are my books.

4 This / These are my pencils.

5 That / Those is Anna's sandwich.

6 Those / That is Malik's phone.

8.3 ÉCRIVEZ CHAQUE PHRASE AU SINGULIER OU AU PLURIEL.

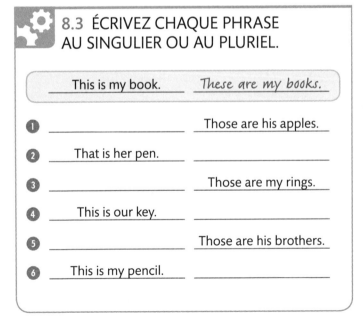

This is my book. | *These are my books.*

1 _____ | Those are his apples.

2 That is her pen. | _____

3 _____ | Those are my rings.

4 This is our key. | _____

5 _____ | Those are his brothers.

6 This is my pencil. | _____

8.4 VOCABULAIRE LES RÈGLES ORTHOGRAPHIQUES DU PLURIEL

Pour la plupart des noms, il suffit d'ajouter un « s » pour former le pluriel.

book

↓

books

Pour les noms se terminant en « x », « ch » et « sh », il faut ajouter « -es ».

watch   **brush**   **box**

↓   ↓   ↓

watches   **brush**es   **box**es

Pour les noms se terminant avec une consonne suivie d'un « y », il faut remplacer le « y » par « -ies ».

dictionary

↓

dictionaries

Aa 8.5 ENTOUREZ 8 PLURIELS DANS LA GRILLE ET CLASSEZ-LES DANS LA BONNE COLONNE.

```
W A T C H E S O B W O A D
A B P X E I N G A Q E P I
N D E M B R U S H E S P A
N E C K L A C E S A C L R
S A N D W I C H E S I E I
D I C T I O N A R I E S E
B O T T L E S Z I S R E S
P Q I W T I O S Y U R D S
T L E L L S H B N E Y S I
```

PLURIELS EN « S » : **PLURIELS EN « ES » :** **PLURIELS EN « IES » :**

❶ _apples_   ❹ _____   ❼ _____

❷ _____   ❺ _____   ❽ _____

❸ _____   ❻ _____

Aa 8.6 ÉCRIVEZ UN NOM PLURIEL POUR DÉCRIRE CHAQUE IMAGE.

 pencils

❸ _____

❻ _____

❶ _____

❹  _____

❼ _____

❷ _____

❺ _____

❽ _____

33

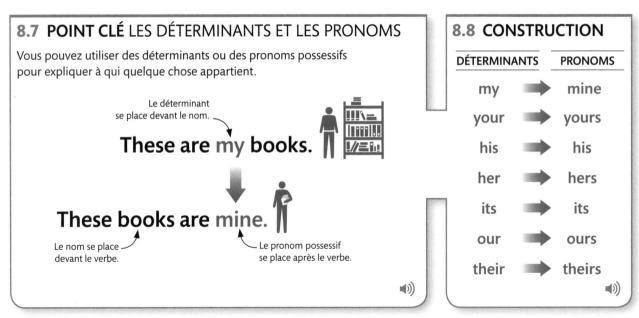

8.7 POINT CLÉ LES DÉTERMINANTS ET LES PRONOMS

Vous pouvez utiliser des déterminants ou des pronoms possessifs pour expliquer à qui quelque chose appartient.

Le déterminant se place devant le nom.

These are my books.

These books are mine.

Le nom se place devant le verbe.

Le pronom possessif se place après le verbe.

8.8 CONSTRUCTION

DÉTERMINANTS		PRONOMS
my	➡	mine
your	➡	yours
his	➡	his
her	➡	hers
its	➡	its
our	➡	ours
their	➡	theirs

8.9 RÉCRIVEZ CHAQUE PHRASE DE 2 FAÇONS DIFFÉRENTES.

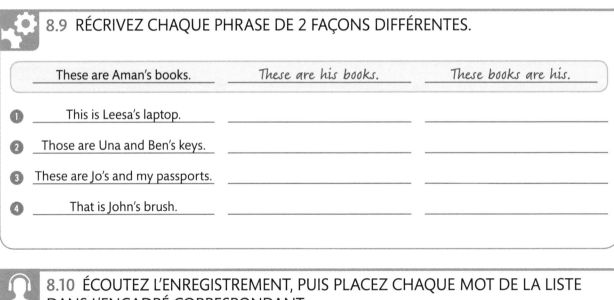

These are Aman's books.	These are his books.	These books are his.

1. This is Leesa's laptop. _____ _____
2. Those are Una and Ben's keys. _____ _____
3. These are Jo's and my passports. _____ _____
4. That is John's brush. _____ _____

8.10 ÉCOUTEZ L'ENREGISTREMENT, PUIS PLACEZ CHAQUE MOT DE LA LISTE DANS L'ENCADRÉ CORRESPONDANT.

Tom et Sarah préparent leurs sacs pour aller au travail.

SAC DE TOM

sandwiches _____
_____ _____

SAC DE SARAH

_____ _____
_____ _____

~~sandwiches~~   ID card

purse   books

chocolate bar   brush

cell phone   notebook

8.11 UTILISEZ LE SCHÉMA POUR CRÉER 12 PHRASES, PUIS LISEZ-LES À VOIX HAUTE.

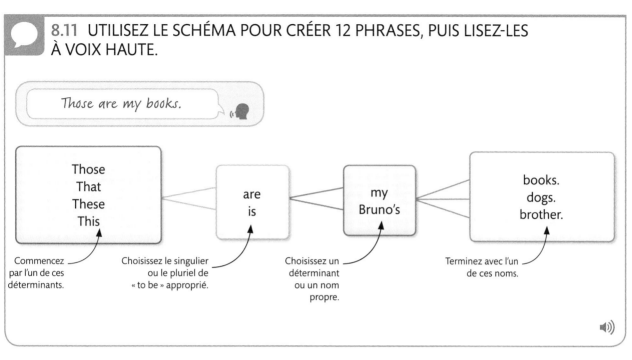

Those are my books.

| Those / That / These / This | are / is | my / Bruno's | books. / dogs. / brother. |

Commencez par l'un de ces déterminants.

Choisissez le singulier ou le pluriel de « to be » approprié.

Choisissez un déterminant ou un nom propre.

Terminez avec l'un de ces noms.

---

08 ✓ CHECK-LIST

⚙ « These » et « those » ☐   **Aa** Vos affaires personnelles ☐   🧩 Les déterminants et les pronoms ☐

↻ BILAN L'ANGLAIS QUE VOUS AVEZ APPRIS DANS LES CHAPITRES 01-08

NOUVEAU POINT LINGUISTIQUE	EXEMPLE TYPE	☑	CHAPITRE
VOUS PRÉSENTER	**Hello!** I am **Joe.** My name is **Joe.**	☐	1.1
QUEL ÂGE AVEZ-VOUS ?	**I'm** 25 years old.	☐	3.1
LES ADJECTIFS POSSESSIFS	**Felix is** my **cat. Coco is** your **rabbit.**	☐	5.1
L'APOSTROPHE AVEC « S »	Lizzie's **mother. Ginger is** my parents' **cat.**	☐	6.1, 6.5
« THIS », « THAT », « THESE » ET « THOSE »	This **is my dog.** That **is my dog.** These **are my bags and** those **are your bags.**	☐	5.6, 8.1
LES DÉTERMINANTS ET LES PRONOMS	**These are** my **books. These books are** mine.	☐	8.7

Vocabulaire

9.1 LES MÉTIERS

cleaner

driver

sales assistant

hairdresser

chef

gardener

vet

actor

doctor

nurse

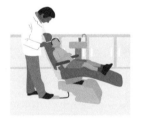

dentist

police officer

fire fighter

farmer

**construction worker (US)
builder (UK)**

artist

receptionist

mechanic

engineer

scientist

teacher

businesswoman

businessman

waiter

waitress

electrician

pilot

judge

9.2 LE PLURIEL DES MÉTIERS

La plupart des noms se rapportant à des personnes ou à des métiers forment leur pluriel de la manière usuelle : on ajoute un « -s » ou « -es ».

driver → **drivers**

waitress → **waitresses**

Les noms se terminant en « -man » deviennent « -men » au pluriel.

man → **men**

woman → **women**

businessman → **businessmen**

businesswoman → **businesswomen**

Pour les noms composés, le second mot est celui qui porte la marque du pluriel.

police officer → **police officers**

37

10 Parler de votre métier

Vous pouvez utiliser le verbe « to be » pour décrire votre métier. Le verbe « to work » (travailler) permet de fournir de plus amples informations sur votre lieu de travail et d'indiquer avec qui vous travaillez.

⚙ **Grammaire** Utiliser « I am » pour parler de votre métier

Aa Vocabulaire Les métiers et les lieux de travail

🧩 **Compétence** Décrire votre métier

10.1 POINT CLÉ VOTRE MÉTIER

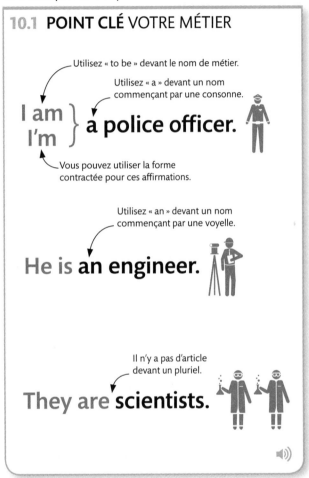

Utilisez « to be » devant le nom de métier.

Utilisez « a » devant un nom commençant par une consonne.

I am
I'm } **a police officer.**

Vous pouvez utiliser la forme contractée pour ces affirmations.

Utilisez « an » devant un nom commençant par une voyelle.

He is an engineer.

Il n'y a pas d'article devant un pluriel.

They are scientists.

10.2 COMPLÉTEZ LES PHRASES EN CONJUGUANT LE VERBE À LA BONNE FORME AVEC L'ARTICLE.

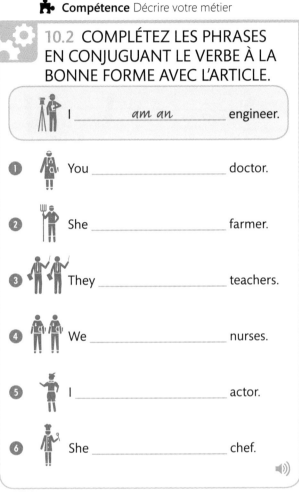

I _____ *am an* _____ engineer.

1. You _____ doctor.

2. She _____ farmer.

3. They _____ teachers.

4. We _____ nurses.

5. I _____ actor.

6. She _____ chef.

10.3 BARREZ LE MOT INCORRECT DANS CHAQUE PHRASE.

They are / ~~is~~ farmers.

1. You **are** / is a driver.

2. I **am** / is a mechanic.

3. He **is** / are a vet.

4. We am / **are** sales assistants.

5. They is / **are** businesswomen.

6. She is / **are** a waitress.

7. We is / **are** receptionists.

8. She **is** / are a gardener.

10.4 **VOCABULAIRE** LES LIEUX DE TRAVAIL

farm

office

theater (US)
theatre (UK)

school

laboratory

restaurant

construction site

hospital

Aa 10.5 RELIEZ CHAQUE MÉTIER À SON LIEU DE TRAVAIL.

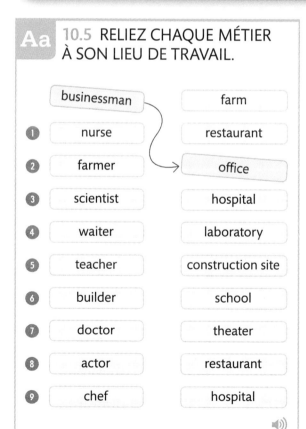

businessman → office

	businessman	farm
1	nurse	restaurant
2	farmer	office
3	scientist	hospital
4	waiter	laboratory
5	teacher	construction site
6	builder	school
7	doctor	theater
8	actor	restaurant
9	chef	hospital

◀))

10.6 **POINT CLÉ** « INSIDE » ET « OUTSIDE »

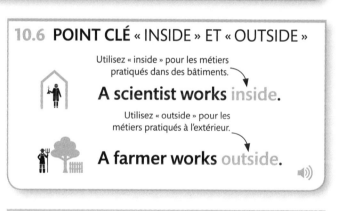

Utilisez « inside » pour les métiers pratiqués dans des bâtiments.

A scientist works inside.

Utilisez « outside » pour les métiers pratiqués à l'extérieur.

A farmer works outside.

◀))

Aa 10.7 COCHEZ LA BONNE RÉPONSE.

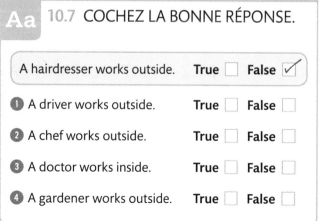

A hairdresser works outside.	**True** ☐	**False** ☑
1 A driver works outside.	**True** ☐	**False** ☐
2 A chef works outside.	**True** ☐	**False** ☐
3 A doctor works inside.	**True** ☐	**False** ☐
4 A gardener works outside.	**True** ☐	**False** ☐

10.8 **POINT CLÉ** « WORK IN » ET « WORK ON »

Utilisez « work in » pour l'emplacement de la plupart des métiers.

I work in **a hospital.**

I work on **a farm.** I work on **construction sites.**

Utilisez « work on » pour parler des fermes et des chantiers de construction.

10.9 ÉCOUTEZ L'ENREGISTREMENT, PUIS NUMÉROTEZ LES IMAGES DANS LE BON ORDRE.

A ☐

C 1

E ☐

B ☐

D ☐

F ☐

10.10 RÉDIGEZ 2 PHRASES POUR DÉCRIRE CHAQUE IMAGE.

Tom _is a farmer._
He works on a farm.

2 We _____

4 He _____

1 She _____

3 You _____

5 Chloe _____

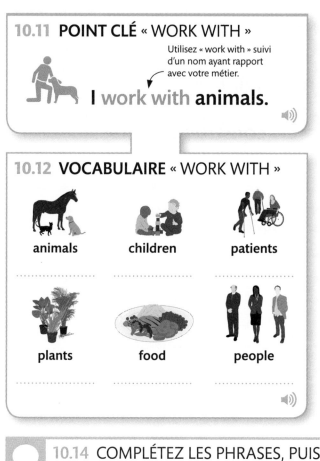

10.11 POINT CLÉ « WORK WITH »

Utilisez « work with » suivi d'un nom ayant rapport avec votre métier.

I work with animals.

10.12 VOCABULAIRE « WORK WITH »

animals

children

patients

plants

food

people

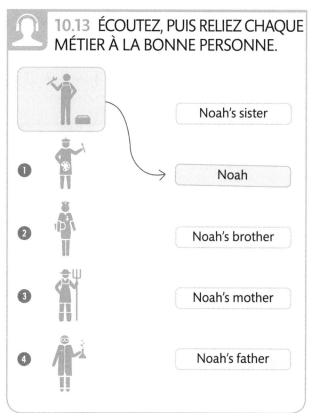

10.13 ÉCOUTEZ, PUIS RELIEZ CHAQUE MÉTIER À LA BONNE PERSONNE.

Noah's sister

Noah

Noah's brother

Noah's mother

Noah's father

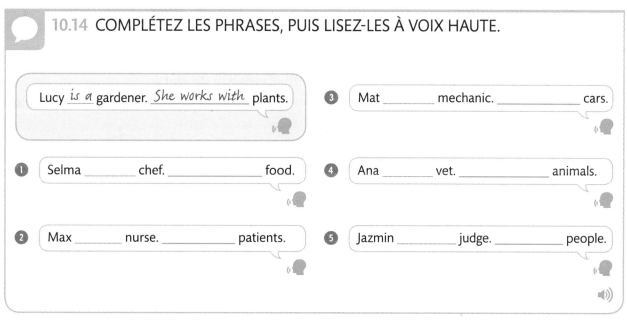

10.14 COMPLÉTEZ LES PHRASES, PUIS LISEZ-LES À VOIX HAUTE.

Lucy *is a* gardener. *She works with* plants.

❶ Selma _____ chef. _____ food.

❷ Max _____ nurse. _____ patients.

❸ Mat _____ mechanic. _____ cars.

❹ Ana _____ vet. _____ animals.

❺ Jazmin _____ judge. _____ people.

11 Dire l'heure

Il existe 2 manières de dire l'heure en anglais.
Vous pouvez utiliser les heures et les minutes,
ou dire les minutes en premier et préciser ensuite
leur relation à l'heure.

⚙ **Grammaire** L'heure
Aa Vocabulaire Le vocabulaire du temps
🧩 **Compétence** Dire l'heure qu'il est

11.1 POINT CLÉ DIRE L'HEURE

Utilisez le verbe « to be »
lorsque vous demandez
ou donnez l'heure.

What time is it?

It's five. It's five o'clock.

It's five fifteen. It's a quarter **past** five.

It's five thirty. It's half **past** five.

It's five forty-five. It's a quarter **to** six.

Vous pouvez omettre
le « a » devant « quarter ».

It's six twenty-three. `06:23`

🔊

11.2 VOCABULAIRE LES HEURES

 midnight

noon

 3 am

 3 pm

🔊

42

11.3 RELIEZ CHAQUE HORLOGE À L'HEURE CORRESPONDANTE.

It's midnight.

0 12:00 → It's seven o'clock.

2 It's two thirty.

3 11:45 It's half past three.

4 It's ten thirty.

5 09:15 It's quarter to twelve.

6 It's a quarter past nine.

11.4 ÉCOUTEZ, PUIS COCHEZ LES HEURES QUE VOUS ENTENDEZ.

5:45 ✓ 6:15 ☐   **3** 03:45 ☐ 04:15 ☐

1 10:30 ☐ 11:30 ☐   **4** 09:30 ☐ 09:45 ☐

2 07:00 ☐ 07:15 ☐   **5** 01:45 ☐ 02:15 ☐

11.6 ÉCRIVEZ LES HEURES EN TOUTES LETTRES, PUIS LISEZ-LES À VOIX HAUTE.

09:15 It's quarter past nine.

1 05:30

2 06:45

3 11:35

4 08:15

5 10:22

11.5 ÉCRIVEZ LES HEURES EN CHIFFRES.

It's a quarter to five. = 4:45

1 It's nine o'clock. = _____

2 It's one fifteen. = _____

3 It's three twenty-five. = _____

4 It's half past two. = _____

5 It's a quarter past twelve. = _____

---

11 ✓ **CHECK-LIST**

⚙ L'heure ☐   **Aa** Le vocabulaire du temps ☐   🧩 Dire l'heure qu'il est ☐

12.1 LES ROUTINES QUOTIDIENNES

wake up

get up

**take a shower (US)
have a shower (UK)**

**take a bath (US)
have a bath (UK)**

brush your hair

**have breakfast /
eat breakfast**

go to work

go to school

buy groceries

go home

cook dinner

**have dinner /
eat dinner**

12.2 LES MOMENTS DE LA JOURNÉE

day

night

dawn

morning

iron a shirt

get dressed

brush your teeth

wash your face

start work

have lunch /
eat lunch

finish work

leave work

clear the table

do the dishes (US)
wash the dishes (UK)

walk the dog

go to bed

afternoon

dusk

evening

late evening

13 Décrire votre journée

Utilisez le présent simple pour parler de choses que vous faites régulièrement : par exemple, l'heure à laquelle vous allez travailler ou manger.

⚙️ **Grammaire** Le présent simple
Aa Vocabulaire Les actions de la routine quotidienne
🧩 **Compétence** Parler de votre routine quotidienne

13.1 POINT CLÉ LE PRÉSENT SIMPLE

Pour former le présent simple, utilisez le radical du verbe (l'infinitif sans « to »).

Le radical du verbe « to eat ».

I eat lunch at noon every day.

She eats lunch at 2pm every day.

Avec « he », « she » et « it », ajoutez « -s » au radical.

13.2 AUTRES EXEMPLES LE PRÉSENT SIMPLE

You get up at 7 o'clock.

We start work at 9 o'clock.

They leave work at 5pm.

She gets up at 5:30am.

He starts work at 11am.

Rob leaves work at 7pm.

13.3 CONSTRUCTION LE PRÉSENT SIMPLE

Le radical du verbe.

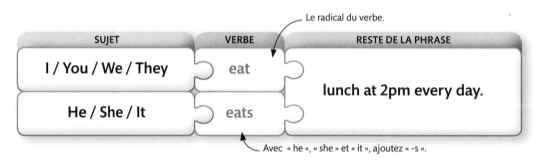

SUJET	VERBE	RESTE DE LA PHRASE
I / You / We / They	eat	lunch at 2pm every day.
He / She / It	eats	

Avec « he », « she » et « it », ajoutez « -s ».

13.4 BARREZ LE MOT INCORRECT DANS CHAQUE PHRASE.

She ~~eat~~ / eats dinner in the evening.

1 He wake up / wakes up at 7 o'clock.

2 You leave / leaves home at 8:30am.

3 I start / starts work at 10am.

4 Ellen get / gets up at 5 o'clock.

5 My wife take / takes a shower in the evening.

6 I take / takes a shower in the morning.

7 My parents eat / eats lunch at 2pm.

8 We leave / leaves work at 4pm.

9 My brother work / works with animals.

🔊

13.5 COMPLÉTEZ LES PHRASES AVEC LES MOTS DE LA LISTE.

Michael _____gets_____ up at 7am.

1 I _____ work at 5:30pm.

2 Phil _____ lunch at 12:30pm.

3 We _____ up at 8am.

4 His son _____ work at 5am.

5 My sister _____ work at 7pm.

6 They _____ dinner at 10pm.

~~gets~~   get   starts

leaves   eat   eats   leave

🔊

13.6 COMPLÉTEZ LES PHRASES, PUIS LISEZ-LES À VOIX HAUTE.

Santiago _____gets_____ (get) up at 6am.

1 My son _____ (wake) up at 5am.

2 I _____ (leave) work at 6:30pm.

3 We _____ (eat) breakfast at 8am.

4 Paula _____ (work) outside.

5 My wife _____ (start) work at 7am.

6 He _____ (eat) lunch at noon.

🔊

13.7 POINT CLÉ LES TERMINAISONS EN « -S » ET « -ES »

Avec certains verbes, on ajoute « -es » avec « he », « she » et « it ». C'est le cas avec les verbes se terminant en « -sh », « -ch », « -o », « -ss », « -x » et « -z ».

I eat lunch

She eats lunch

Pour la plupart des verbes, on ajoute simplement « -s ».

I finish work

He finishes work

Ajoutez « -es » aux verbes se terminant en « -sh ».

I watch TV

She watches TV

Ajoutez « -es » aux verbes se terminant en « -ch ».

13.8 PRONONCIATION DIRE « -S » ET « -ES »

Les terminaisons en « -s » ont différentes prononciations. Écoutez les différences.

eats

Un son « s ».

leaves

Un son « z ».

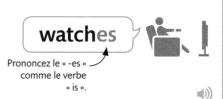

watches

Prononcez le « -es » comme le verbe « is ».

13.9 LISEZ LES MOTS À VOIX HAUTE.

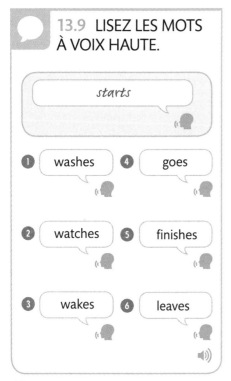

starts

1 washes   4 goes

2 watches   5 finishes

3 wakes   6 leaves

13.10 COMPLÉTEZ LES PHRASES EN CONJUGUANT CORRECTEMENT LES VERBES.

He ___finishes___ (finish) work at 5 o'clock.

1 Lucia _____ (wake) up at 7am.

2 I _____ (get) up at 7:30am.

3 Ethan _____ (go) to work at 5am.

4 You _____ (leave) work at 5pm.

5 Shona _____ (watch) TV in the evening.

13.11 RÉCRIVEZ LES PHRASES EN CORRIGEANT LES ERREURS.

Our children **eats** breakfast at 8am.
Our children eat breakfast at 8am.

❶ My mother **watchs** TV in the morning.

_____

❷ We **goes** to bed at midnight.

_____

❸ My husband **finishs** work at 6:30pm.

_____

❹ Rob **go** to work at 8:30am.

_____

❺ I **takes** a shower in the morning.

_____

❻ I **leaves** work at 6 o'clock in the evening.

_____

13.12 ÉCOUTEZ ET RÉPONDEZ AUX QUESTIONS.

Joan parle de sa routine quotidienne et de son emploi du temps.

She starts work at 4pm.
True ☐ **False** ☑

❶ She finishes work at 12pm.
True ☐ **False** ☐

❷ She eats lunch at 1pm.
True ☐ **False** ☐

❸ She has dinner at 7:30pm.
True ☐ **False** ☐

❹ She watches TV in the afternoon.
True ☐ **False** ☐

❺ She goes on the computer in the evening.
True ☐ **False** ☐

❻ She goes to bed at 8:30pm.
True ☐ **False** ☐

13.13 UTILISEZ LE SCHÉMA POUR CRÉER 12 PHRASES, PUIS LISEZ-LES À VOIX HAUTE.

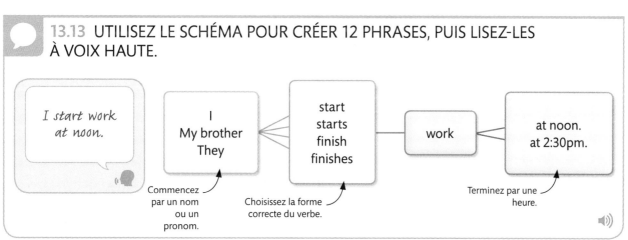

I start work at noon.

I
My brother
They

start
starts
finish
finishes

work

at noon.
at 2:30pm.

Commencez par un nom ou un pronom.

Choisissez la forme correcte du verbe.

Terminez par une heure.

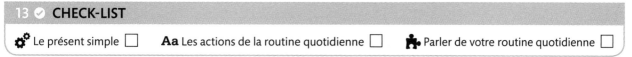

13 ✓ **CHECK-LIST**

⚙ Le présent simple ☐   **Aa** Les actions de la routine quotidienne ☐   🧩 Parler de votre routine quotidienne ☐

14 Décrire votre semaine

Vous pouvez parler de vos activités hebdomadaires habituelles en utilisant le présent simple et des expressions de temps. Celles-ci sont généralement formées avec des prépositions et des jours de la semaine.

🔧 **Grammaire** Les jours et les prépositions
Aa Vocabulaire Les jours de la semaine
🧩 **Compétence** Parler de votre routine hebdomadaire

14.1 VOCABULAIRE LES JOURS DE LA SEMAINE

weekend

MON	TUE	WED	THU	FRI	SAT	SUN
Monday	Tuesday	Wednesday	Thursday	Friday	Saturday	Sunday

🔊

14.2 POINT CLÉ LES PRÉPOSITIONS ET LES JOURS DE LA SEMAINE

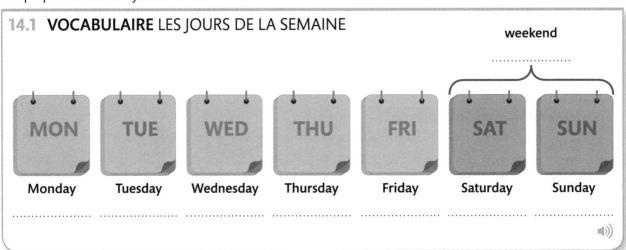

Utilisez « on » devant le jour de la semaine pour parler du jour où vous faites quelque chose.

Vous devez ajouter « -s » au jour de la semaine pour indiquer que quelque chose a lieu régulièrement ce jour-là.

I go to work on Mondays.

I work from Monday to Friday.

Utilisez « from » pour indiquer le jour où vous commencez quelque chose.

Utilisez « to » pour indiquer le jour où vous terminez quelque chose.

CONSEIL
Aux États-Unis, vous pouvez également omettre « go to » et la préposition lorsque vous parlez des jours où vous travaillez : « I work Mondays. »

« On the weekend » est plus fréquent aux États-Unis.

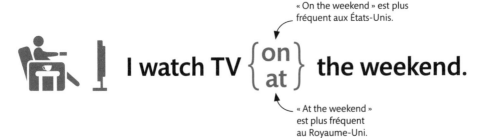

I watch TV { on / at } the weekend.

« At the weekend » est plus fréquent au Royaume-Uni.

🔊

14.3 COMPLÉTEZ LES PHRASES AVEC LA PRÉPOSITION APPROPRIÉE.

Sharon wakes up at 5am __on__ Mondays.

1 We eat lunch at 3pm _____ the weekend.

2 She goes to bed at 1am _____ the weekend.

3 I go to work _____ Monday _____ Wednesday.

4 They eat dinner at 9pm _____ the weekend.

5 We finish work at 3pm _____ Fridays.

6 I eat breakfast at work _____ Mondays.

🔊

14.4 VOCABULAIRE LES ACTIVITÉS

| go to the gym | go swimming | play tennis | play soccer | read the newspaper | take a bath |

🔊

Aa 14.5 OBSERVEZ LES IMAGES, PUIS COMPLÉTEZ LES PHRASES.

She _plays tennis_ on Mondays.

1 He _____ on Tuesdays and Fridays.

2 They _____ on Thursdays.

3 He _____ on Wednesdays.

4 I _____ on the weekend.

5 You _____ on Saturdays.

🔊

14.6 COMPLÉTEZ LES PHRASES, PUIS LISEZ-LES À VOIX HAUTE.

I play tennis _____on_____ Wednesdays.

1 I watch TV _____ Sundays.

2 I take a bath _____ 7pm every day.

3 I go to bed ____ 10 o'clock ____ Sundays.

4 I get up ____ 8am ____ Monday to Friday.

🔊

14.7 VOCABULAIRE LES EXPRESSIONS DE FRÉQUENCE

Utilisez les expressions de fréquence pour indiquer la fréquence à laquelle quelque chose se produit.

once a week

twice a week

three times a week

every day

14.8 CONSTRUCTION LES EXPRESSIONS DE FRÉQUENCE

L'expression de fréquence se place généralement à la fin de la phrase.

PRÉSENT SIMPLE	FRÉQUENCE
I go to the gym	**twice a week.**

14.9 AUTRES EXEMPLES LES EXPRESSIONS DE FRÉQUENCE

He goes to work three times a week.

She goes swimming four times a week.

We eat dinner at 7:30pm every day.

They watch TV five times a week.

14.10 ÉCOUTEZ L'ENREGISTREMENT, PUIS COCHEZ LES BONNES RÉPONSES.

Angela wakes up at 5:30am every day.
True ☐ **False** ☑

1 Fred works from 8am to 6pm five times a week.
True ☐ **False** ☐

2 Scott has dinner at 6am.
True ☐ **False** ☐

3 Linda has a shower every morning.
True ☐ **False** ☐

4 Jennifer watches TV on the weekend.
True ☐ **False** ☐

5 Tim's daughter goes to bed at 7:30pm on Sundays.
True ☐ **False** ☐

14.11 ÉCRIVEZ LES MOTS DANS LE BON ORDRE AFIN DE RECONSTITUER LES PHRASES.

every | day. | a shower | has | He

He has a shower every day.

1 get up | five days | I | at 6am | a week.

_____

2 every | day. | They | at 11pm | go to bed

_____

3 plays | soccer | Sarah | twice a week.

_____

4 once | his clothes | a week. | washes | Jamie

_____

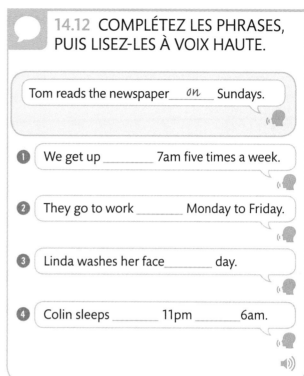

14.12 COMPLÉTEZ LES PHRASES, PUIS LISEZ-LES À VOIX HAUTE.

Tom reads the newspaper___*on*___ Sundays.

1 We get up _____ 7am five times a week.

2 They go to work _____ Monday to Friday.

3 Linda washes her face_____ day.

4 Colin sleeps _____ 11pm _____6am.

14 ✓ CHECK-LIST

⚙ Les jours et les prépositions ☐   **Aa** Les jours de la semaine ☐   🧩 Parler de votre routine hebdomadaire ☐

🔄 BILAN L'ANGLAIS QUE VOUS AVEZ APPRIS DANS LES CHAPITRES 10-14

NOUVEAU POINT LINGUISTIQUE	EXEMPLE TYPE	☑	CHAPITRE
PARLER DE VOTRE MÉTIER	I am **a police officer.** He is **an engineer.**	☐	10.1
« WORK IN », « WORK ON » ET « WORK WITH »	I work in **a hospital.** I work on **a farm.** I work with **animals.**	☐	10.8, 10.11
DIRE L'HEURE	It's **five.** It's **five o'clock.**	☐	11.1, 11.2
LE PRÉSENT SIMPLE	I eat **lunch at noon every day.** She eats **lunch at 2pm every day.**	☐	13.1
LES PRÉPOSITIONS ET LES JOURS DE LA SEMAINE	I work on **Mondays.** I work from **Monday** to **Friday.**	☐	14.2
LES EXPRESSIONS DE FRÉQUENCE	I go to the gym **twice a week.**	☐	14.8, 14.9

15 « To be » à la forme négative

Pour former une phrase négative, vous devez utiliser « not » ou sa forme contractée « n't ». Les règles pour les phrases négatives avec le verbe « to be » sont différentes de celles pour les phrases négatives avec d'autres verbes.

⚙ **Grammaire** « To be » à la forme négative

Aa Vocabulaire « Not »

🧩 **Compétence** Dire ce que les choses ne sont pas

15.1 POINT CLÉ LA FORME NÉGATIVE DU VERBE « TO BE »

Ajoutez « not » après « to be » pour construire une phrase négative.

I am **a farmer.** I am **not a doctor.**

On ajoute « not » pour construire une phrase négative.

🔊

15.2 AUTRES EXEMPLES LA FORME NÉGATIVE DU VERBE « TO BE »

 He is **not an adult.**

 It is **not 5 o'clock.**

 They are **not engineers.**

 This is **not a pig.**

 We are **not actors.**

 That is **not my bag.**

🔊

15.3 CONSTRUCTION LA FORME NÉGATIVE DU VERBE « TO BE »

Le verbe « to be » se conjugue de la même manière à la forme négative et à la forme affirmative. Il suffit d'ajouter « not » à la forme négative.

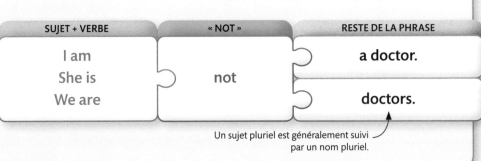

SUJET + VERBE	« NOT »	RESTE DE LA PHRASE
I am She is We are	not	a doctor. doctors.

Un sujet pluriel est généralement suivi par un nom pluriel.

15.4 ÉCRIVEZ LES MOTS SUIVANTS DANS LE BON ORDRE AFIN DE RECONSTITUER LES PHRASES.

gardener. | Jack | not | is | a

Jack is not a gardener.

3 years | I | old. | not | am | 35

_____

1 sister. | my | She | not | is

_____

4 are | not | Spanish. | We

_____

2 her | not | car. | is | That

_____

5 vet. | Chad | a | not | is

_____

🔊

15.5 COMPLÉTEZ LES PHRASES POUR FORMER UNE PHRASE NÉGATIVE.

It _____ *is not* _____ 11 o'clock.

1 He _____ in the office.

2 She _____ a businesswoman.

3 I _____ 18 years old.

4 This _____ a snake.

5 We _____ artists.

6 You _____ at work.

7 Dexter _____ a cat.

🔊

15.6 ÉCOUTEZ L'ENREGISTREMENT, PUIS NUMÉROTEZ LES IMAGES DANS LE BON ORDRE.

Ⓐ ☐ Ⓑ 1 Ⓒ ☐ Ⓓ ☐ Ⓔ ☐

15.7 POINT CLÉ LES FORMES NÉGATIVES CONTRACTÉES

Vous pouvez contracter « you are not » de 2 façons. Vous pouvez contracter le sujet et le verbe, ou le verbe et « not ».

La forme contractée de « you are » est « you're ».

You are not a doctor.

You're not
You aren't } **a doctor.**

La forme contractée de « are not » est « aren't ».

15.8 AUTRES EXEMPLES LES FORMES NÉGATIVES CONTRACTÉES

I am not **a teacher.**

I'm not **a teacher.**

Vous ne pouvez pas dire « I amn't ».

He is not **a farmer.**

He's not
He isn't } **a farmer.**

She is not **American.**

She's not
She isn't } **American.**

It is not **a pencil.**

It's not
It isn't } **a pencil.**

We are not **waiters.**

We're not
We aren't } **waiters.**

They are not **British.**

They're not
They aren't } **British.**

15.9 RÉCRIVEZ LES PHRASES SUIVANTES EN CORRIGEANT LES ERREURS.

Louis aren't Hayley's uncle.
Louis isn't Hayley's uncle.

1 It am not 10 o'clock in the morning.
_____

2 You isn't 35 years old.
_____

3 I aren't Australian.
_____

4 My brother aren't married.
_____

5 Tom and Angela isn't construction workers.
_____

15.10 LISEZ LE BLOG, PUIS COCHEZ LES BONNES RÉPONSES.

Françoise is 33 years old.
True ☐ **False** ☑

❶ She isn't from the USA.
True ☐ **False** ☐

❷ She speaks French.
True ☐ **False** ☐

❸ She is French.
True ☐ **False** ☐

❹ Her husband speaks English.
True ☐ **False** ☐

❺ Her husband is British.
True ☐ **False** ☐

❻ They live in the USA.
True ☐ **False** ☐

❼ Her husband isn't a student.
True ☐ **False** ☐

My life Blog

HOME | ENTRIES | ABOUT | CONTACT

POSTED TUESDAY, OCTOBER 16
ABOUT ME

My name is Françoise, and I'm 35 years old. I speak French, but I'm not from France. I'm from Québec. I'm married to a man called Henry. He speaks English, but he isn't from North America and he isn't from Britain. He's from New Zealand. We don't live in Québec or New Zealand. We live in Ohio, USA. We are graduate students there.

15.11 UTILISEZ LE SCHÉMA POUR CRÉER 12 PHRASES, PUIS LISEZ-LES À VOIX HAUTE.

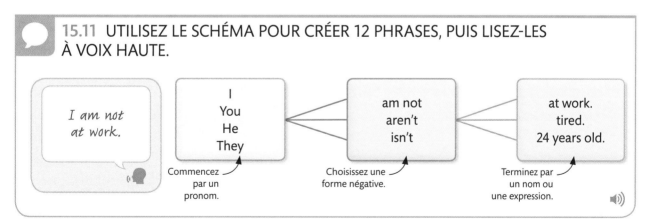

I am not at work.

| I You He They | am not aren't isn't | at work. tired. 24 years old. |

Commencez par un pronom.

Choisissez une forme négative.

Terminez par un nom ou une expression.

15 ⊘ CHECK-LIST

⚙ « To be » à la forme négative ☐   **Aa** « Not » ☐   🧩 Dire ce que les choses ne sont pas ☐

16 Les autres négations

Pour mettre le présent à la forme négative, il suffit d'ajouter « do not » ou « does not » devant la plupart des verbes. Ces formes sont souvent contractées en « don't » ou « doesn't ».

⚙ **Grammaire** Le présent simple à la forme négative

Aa Vocabulaire Les activités quotidiennes

🧩 **Compétence** Dire ce que vous ne faites pas

16.1 POINT CLÉ LE PRÉSENT SIMPLE À LA FORME NÉGATIVE

Ajoutez « do not » devant le verbe pour former la négation avec « I », « you », « we » ou « they ». Après « he », « she » ou « it », utilisez « does not ».

I work outside.

Le verbe principal ne change pas.

⬇

I do not work outside.
I work inside.

He works inside.

⬇

He does not work inside.
He works outside.

🔊

16.2 AUTRES EXEMPLES LE PRÉSENT SIMPLE À LA FORME NÉGATIVE

 You do not have a laptop.

 We do not start work at 8am.

 He does not live in Los Angeles.

 The house does not have a backyard.

 🔊

16.3 CONSTRUCTION LE PRÉSENT SIMPLE À LA FORME NÉGATIVE

Utilisez « do » ou « does » avec « not » suivi du radical (infinitif sans « to ») du verbe principal.

SUJET	« DO/DOES » + « NOT »	RADICAL	RESTE DE LA PHRASE
I / You / We / They	do not	work	outside.
He / She / It	does not		

16.4 COMPLÉTEZ LES PHRASES EN UTILISANT « DO NOT » OU « DOES NOT ».

She _does not_ go to the gym on Thursdays.

1. I _____ read the papers on Saturday.

2. The dog _____ eat fish.

3. They _____ go to the theater often.

4. Ben and I _____ live on a farm now.

5. Theo _____ cycle to work.

6. You _____ work at Fabio's café.

7. Claire _____ watch TV in the evening.

8. We _____ play football at home.

9. Pierre _____ wake up before noon.

🔊

16.5 ÉCOUTEZ, PUIS COCHEZ LES BONNES RÉPONSES.

Frank parle de ses routines quotidiennes et hebdomadaires.

Frank works in a store on Queen Street.
True ☑ **False** ☐

1. Frank gets up at 5am.
True ☐ **False** ☐

2. Frank has lunch at 1pm every day.
True ☐ **False** ☐

3. Frank goes swimming on Wednesday evening.
True ☐ **False** ☐

4. Frank watches TV every night before bed.
True ☐ **False** ☐

16.6 POINT CLÉ LA FORME NÉGATIVE CONTRACTÉE

En anglais, les formes « do not » et « does not » sont souvent contractées en « don't » et « doesn't ».

I do not work outside.

I don't work outside.

He does not work outside.

He doesn't work outside.

🔊

16.7 AUTRES EXEMPLES LE PRÉSENT SIMPLE À LA FORME NÉGATIVE : LES FORMES CONTRACTÉES

You don't play soccer.

She doesn't speak English.

We don't want that cake.

He doesn't live near here.

🔊

16.8 RÉCRIVEZ LA PHRASE DE 2 MANIÈRES DIFFÉRENTES.

| I get up at 7am. | I do not get up at 7am. | I don't get up at 7am. |

1 _____ | _____ | We don't go to work every day.

2 _____ | He does not watch TV in the evening. | _____

3 You work in an office. | _____ | _____

4 _____ | _____ | They don't play tennis.

5 _____ | She does not work with children. | _____

 16.9 RÉCRIVEZ LES PHRASES SUIVANTES EN CORRIGEANT LES ERREURS.

He **don't** play soccer on Saturdays.
He doesn't play soccer on Saturdays.

1 We **doesn't** work with animals.

_____

2 I **doesn't** eat chocolate.

_____

3 Sandy **don't** work in a hairdresser's.

_____

4 Melanie and Cris **doesn't** have a car.

_____

5 They **doesn't** live in Park Road now.

_____

6 We **doesn't** watch Hollywood movies.

_____

7 She **don't** drive a taxi.

_____

◀))

16.10 UTILISEZ LE SCHÉMA POUR CRÉER 12 PHRASES, PUIS LISEZ-LES À VOIX HAUTE.

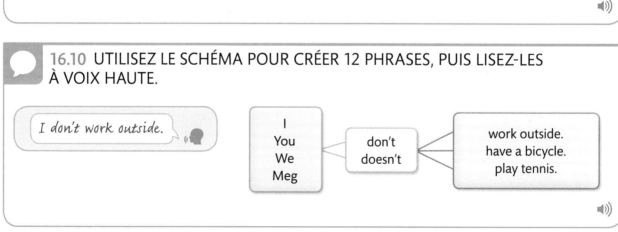

I don't work outside.

| I
You
We
Meg | don't
doesn't | work outside.
have a bicycle.
play tennis. |

◀))

16.11 LISEZ L'ARTICLE SUIVANT, PUIS COCHEZ LES BONNES RÉPONSES.

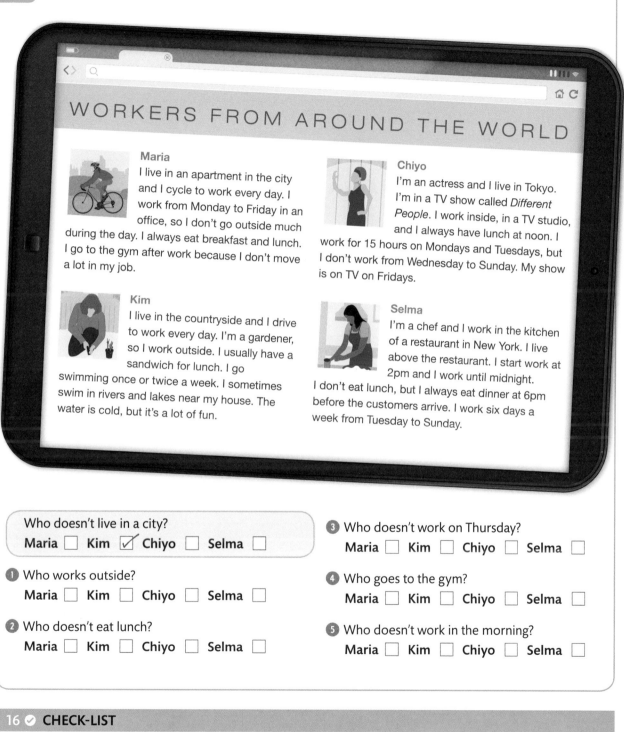

WORKERS FROM AROUND THE WORLD

Maria
I live in an apartment in the city and I cycle to work every day. I work from Monday to Friday in an office, so I don't go outside much during the day. I always eat breakfast and lunch. I go to the gym after work because I don't move a lot in my job.

Chiyo
I'm an actress and I live in Tokyo. I'm in a TV show called *Different People*. I work inside, in a TV studio, and I always have lunch at noon. I work for 15 hours on Mondays and Tuesdays, but I don't work from Wednesday to Sunday. My show is on TV on Fridays.

Kim
I live in the countryside and I drive to work every day. I'm a gardener, so I work outside. I usually have a sandwich for lunch. I go swimming once or twice a week. I sometimes swim in rivers and lakes near my house. The water is cold, but it's a lot of fun.

Selma
I'm a chef and I work in the kitchen of a restaurant in New York. I live above the restaurant. I start work at 2pm and I work until midnight. I don't eat lunch, but I always eat dinner at 6pm before the customers arrive. I work six days a week from Tuesday to Sunday.

Who doesn't live in a city?
Maria ☐ **Kim** ☐ **Chiyo** ☑ **Selma** ☐

1 Who works outside?
Maria ☐ **Kim** ☐ **Chiyo** ☐ **Selma** ☐

2 Who doesn't eat lunch?
Maria ☐ **Kim** ☐ **Chiyo** ☐ **Selma** ☐

3 Who doesn't work on Thursday?
Maria ☐ **Kim** ☐ **Chiyo** ☐ **Selma** ☐

4 Who goes to the gym?
Maria ☐ **Kim** ☐ **Chiyo** ☐ **Selma** ☐

5 Who doesn't work in the morning?
Maria ☐ **Kim** ☐ **Chiyo** ☐ **Selma** ☐

---

16 ✓ CHECK-LIST

⚙ Le présent simple à la forme négative ☐   **Aa** Les activités quotidiennes ☐   🧩 Dire ce que vous ne faites pas ☐

17 Les questions simples

Pour poser des questions simples avec le verbe
« to be », il suffit de changer l'ordre du sujet et du verbe.
La réponse à une question simple commence
généralement par « yes » ou « no ».

⚙ **Grammaire** Les questions simples
Aa Vocabulaire Les métiers et les activités de routine
🧩 **Compétence** Poser des questions simples

17.1 POINT CLÉ LES QUESTIONS AVEC « TO BE »

Pour poser une
question avec le verbe
« to be », il suffit
de placer le verbe
avant le sujet.

Dans une affirmation, le sujet
se place devant le verbe.

You are Canadian.

Are you Canadian?

Dans une question, le verbe
se place en début de phrase.

Le sujet se place après le verbe.

17.2 AUTRES EXEMPLES LES QUESTIONS AVEC « TO BE »

Is Judi **an actor?**

Is he **French?**

Are they **engineers?**

Are you **a student?**

17.3 CONSTRUCTION LES QUESTIONS AVEC « TO BE »

« TO BE »	SUJET	RESTE DE LA PHRASE
Am	I	
Are	you / we / they	Canadian?
Is	he / she / it	

17.4 RÉCRIVEZ LES PHRASES SUIVANTES À LA FORME INTERROGATIVE.

She is a gardener.
Is she a gardener?

1 Brad is a nurse.

_____

2 These are my keys.

_____

3 Ruby and Farid are actors.

_____

4 This is his laptop.

_____

5 Valeria is his sister.

_____

🔊

17.5 ÉCOUTEZ L'ENREGISTREMENT, PUIS ENTOUREZ LA BONNE RÉPONSE.

17.6 INTONATION LES QUESTIONS SIMPLES

En anglais, la voix monte généralement à la fin des phrases interrogatives simples.

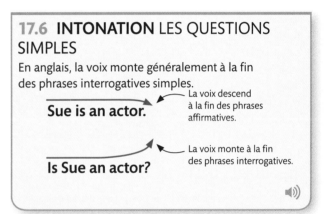

Sue is an actor. — La voix descend à la fin des phrases affirmatives.

Is Sue an actor? — La voix monte à la fin des phrases interrogatives.

🔊

17.7 COMPLÉTEZ LES PHRASES, PUIS LISEZ-LES À VOIX HAUTE.

_____*Is*_____ she a waitress?

1 _____ Holly your mother?

2 _____ they from Argentina?

3 _____ you a teacher?

4 _____ this your dog?

5 _____ there a post office?

🔊

17.8 POINT CLÉ LES QUESTIONS AVEC « DO » ET « DOES »

Pour poser une question sans le verbe « to be », commencez la question avec « do » ou « does ».

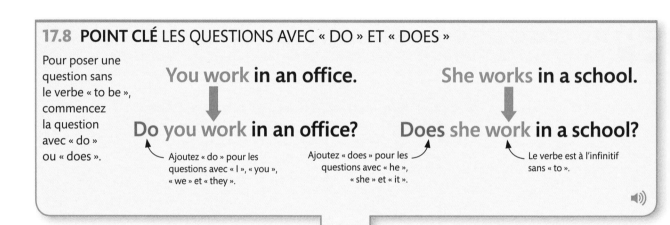

You work **in an office.**

Do you work **in an office?**

Ajoutez « do » pour les questions avec « I », « you », « we » et « they ».

She works **in a school.**

Does she work **in a school?**

Ajoutez « does » pour les questions avec « he », « she » et « it ».

Le verbe est à l'infinitif sans « to ».

17.9 AUTRES EXEMPLES LES QUESTIONS AVEC « DO » ET « DOES »

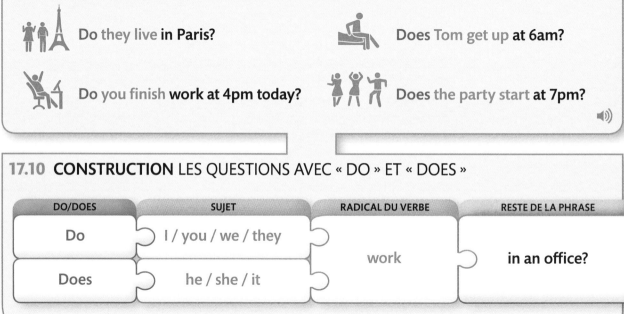

Do they live **in Paris?**

Does Tom get up **at 6am?**

Do you finish **work at 4pm today?**

Does the party start **at 7pm?**

17.10 CONSTRUCTION LES QUESTIONS AVEC « DO » ET « DOES »

DO/DOES	SUJET	RADICAL DU VERBE	RESTE DE LA PHRASE
Do	I / you / we / they	work	in an office?
Does	he / she / it		

17.11 COMPLÉTEZ LES QUESTIONS AVEC « DO » OU « DOES ».

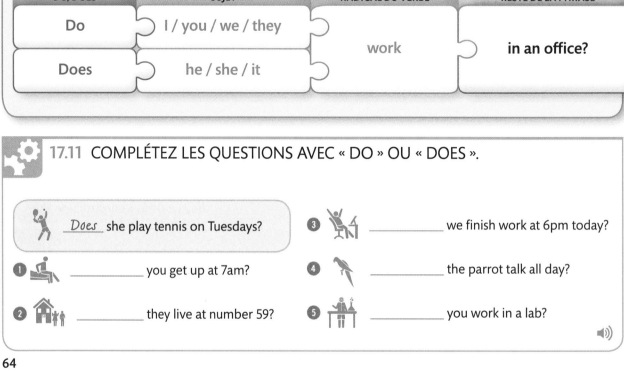

Does she play tennis on Tuesdays?

❸ _____ we finish work at 6pm today?

❶ _____ you get up at 7am?

❹ _____ the parrot talk all day?

❷ _____ they live at number 59?

❺ _____ you work in a lab?

64

17.12 ÉCRIVEZ LES MOTS SUIVANTS DANS LE BON ORDRE AFIN DE RECONSTITUER LES PHRASES.

go swimming | Jin | Does | on Fridays?

Does Jin go swimming on Fridays?

3 get up | he | Does | at 5am | every day?

_____

1 in New York? | live | you | Do

_____

4 come | Peru? | they | Do | from

_____

2 on a farm? | Does | work | she

_____

5 work | Brad | Does | in the post office?

_____

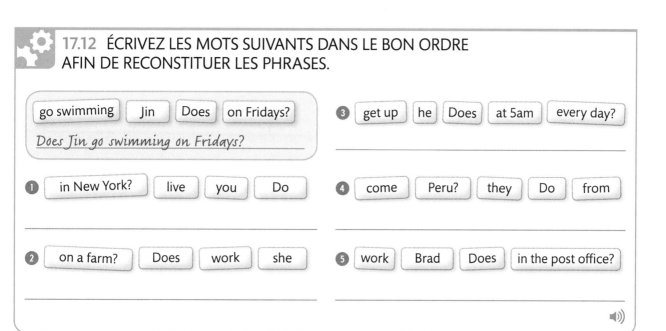

17.13 ÉCRIVEZ LES PHRASES À LA FORME INTERROGATIVE.

Kim goes to work at 8am.

Does Kim go to work at 8am?

1 They live in New York City.

_____

2 He works in a restaurant.

_____

3 Lewis goes swimming on Fridays.

_____

4 Marisha works with animals.

_____

17.14 COMPLÉTEZ LES PHRASES, PUIS LISEZ-LES À VOIX HAUTE.

_____Do_____ you play soccer on Fridays?

1 _____ she go swimming on Tuesdays?

2 _____ you read the paper on Sundays?

3 _____ she work with animals?

4 _____ they work on a construction site?

17 ✔ CHECK-LIST

⚙ Les questions simples ☐   **Aa** Les métiers et les activités de routine ☐   🧩 Poser des questions simples ☐

18 Répondre aux questions

Lorsque vous répondez à une question en anglais, vous pouvez omettre des mots afin d'alléger votre réponse. Ces réponses courtes sont souvent utilisées à l'oral.

✿ **Grammaire** Les réponses courtes
Aa Vocabulaire Les métiers et les routines
🧩 **Compétence** Répondre à des questions à l'oral

18.1 POINT CLÉ LES RÉPONSES COURTES

Lorsque le verbe « to be » est utilisé dans la question, utilisez « to be » dans votre réponse courte. Si « do » ou « does » est utilisé dans la question, utilisez « do » ou « does » dans la réponse courte.

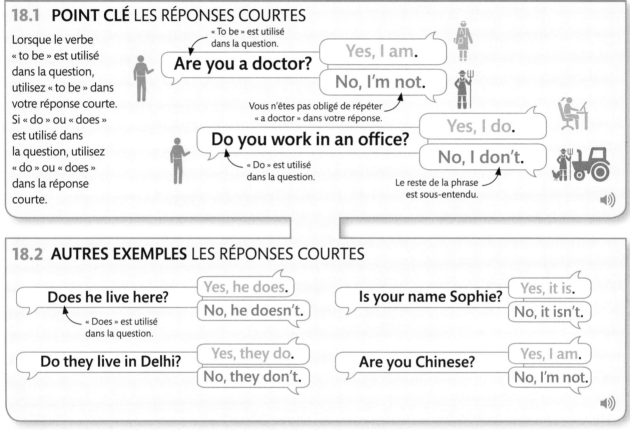

« To be » est utilisé dans la question.

Are you a doctor?

Yes, I am.

No, I'm not.

Vous n'êtes pas obligé de répéter « a doctor » dans votre réponse.

Do you work in an office?

« Do » est utilisé dans la question.

Yes, I do.

No, I don't.

Le reste de la phrase est sous-entendu.

18.2 AUTRES EXEMPLES LES RÉPONSES COURTES

Does he live here?

Yes, he does.

No, he doesn't.

« Does » est utilisé dans la question.

Do they live in Delhi?

Yes, they do.

No, they don't.

Is your name Sophie?

Yes, it is.

No, it isn't.

Are you Chinese?

Yes, I am.

No, I'm not.

18.3 ÉCOUTEZ L'ENREGISTREMENT, PUIS COCHEZ LES BONNES RÉPONSES.

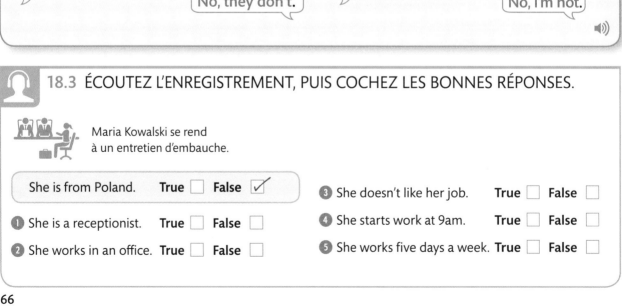

Maria Kowalski se rend à un entretien d'embauche.

She is from Poland. **True** ☐ **False** ☑

❶ She is a receptionist. **True** ☐ **False** ☐

❷ She works in an office. **True** ☐ **False** ☐

❸ She doesn't like her job. **True** ☐ **False** ☐

❹ She starts work at 9am. **True** ☐ **False** ☐

❺ She works five days a week. **True** ☐ **False** ☐

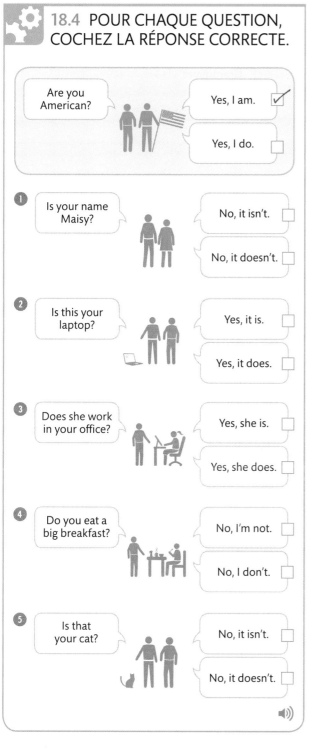

18.4 POUR CHAQUE QUESTION, COCHEZ LA RÉPONSE CORRECTE.

Are you American?

Yes, I am. ✓

Yes, I do. ☐

1 Is your name Maisy?

No, it isn't. ☐

No, it doesn't. ☐

2 Is this your laptop?

Yes, it is. ☐

Yes, it does. ☐

3 Does she work in your office?

Yes, she is. ☐

Yes, she does. ☐

4 Do you eat a big breakfast?

No, I'm not. ☐

No, I don't. ☐

5 Is that your cat?

No, it isn't. ☐

No, it doesn't. ☐

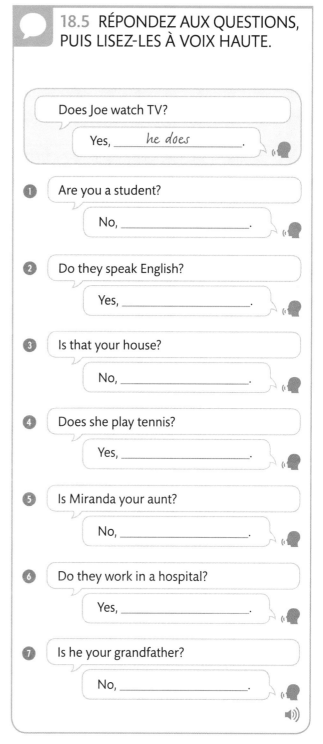

18.5 RÉPONDEZ AUX QUESTIONS, PUIS LISEZ-LES À VOIX HAUTE.

Does Joe watch TV?

Yes, _he does_.

1 Are you a student?

No, _____.

2 Do they speak English?

Yes, _____.

3 Is that your house?

No, _____.

4 Does she play tennis?

Yes, _____.

5 Is Miranda your aunt?

No, _____.

6 Do they work in a hospital?

Yes, _____.

7 Is he your grandfather?

No, _____.

---

18 ✓ CHECK-LIST

⚙ Les réponses courtes ☐   **Aa** Les métiers et les routines ☐   🧩 Répondre à des questions à l'oral ☐

19 Poser des questions

Utilisez des mots interrogatifs tels que « what », « who »,
« when » et « where » pour poser des questions ouvertes
auxquelles on ne peut pas répondre par « yes » ou « no ».

🔧 **Grammaire** Les questions ouvertes
Aa Vocabulaire Les mots interrogatifs
🧩 **Compétence** Demander des précisions

19.1 POINT CLÉ LES QUESTIONS OUVERTES AVEC LE VERBE « TO BE »

Le mot interrogatif
se place au début
de la question. Il est
généralement suivi
par le verbe « to be ».

**My name is Sarah.
What is your name?**

Le mot interrogatif
se place au début.

La question est
« ouverte » car on ne
peut y répondre par
« oui » ou par « non ».

19.2 AUTRES EXEMPLES LES QUESTIONS OUVERTES AVEC LE VERBE « TO BE »

What is Ruby's job?

What is the time?

What is in the bag?

What are we here for?

What is this thing?

What are Elliot's sisters called?

19.3 BARREZ LE MOT INCORRECT DANS CHAQUE PHRASE.

What is / ~~are~~ / ~~am~~ the capital of France?

① What is / are / am their names?

② What is / are / am the time?

③ What is / are / am my favorite colors?

④ What is / are / am the hotel next to?

⑤ What is / are / am they?

⑥ What is / are / am your uncle's name?

⑦ What is / are / am my name?

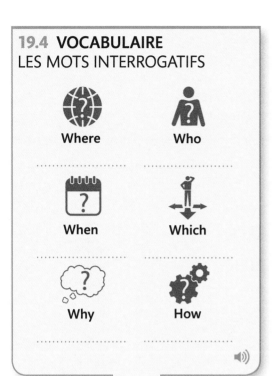

19.4 VOCABULAIRE
LES MOTS INTERROGATIFS

Where

Who

When

Which

Why

How

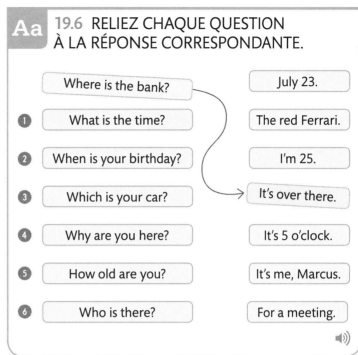

Aa 19.6 RELIEZ CHAQUE QUESTION À LA RÉPONSE CORRESPONDANTE.

Where is the bank?   July 23.

1 What is the time?   The red Ferrari.

2 When is your birthday?   I'm 25.

3 Which is your car?   It's over there.

4 Why are you here?   It's 5 o'clock.

5 How old are you?   It's me, Marcus.

6 Who is there?   For a meeting.

19.5 AUTRES EXEMPLES
LES MOTS INTERROGATIFS

Where is the café?

Who is Jo's teacher?

When is dinner?

Which is your car?

Why am I here?

How are you?

19.7 COMPLÉTEZ LES QUESTIONS AVEC LE MOT INTERROGATIF APPROPRIÉ.

_____*What*_____ is your name?

1 _____ are your parents from?

2 _____ old are you?

3 _____ is breakfast?

4 _____ is your friend talking to?

5 _____ is it cold in here?

6 _____ person is your teacher?

What	Where	Who	When
Which		Why	How

19.8 POINT CLÉ LES QUESTIONS OUVERTES AVEC « DO » ET « DOES »

Avec la plupart des verbes autres que « to be », on utilise le mot interrogatif suivi de « do » ou « does » pour formuler une question.

« Do » ou « does » suit le mot interrogatif.

When do you eat lunch?

Le mot interrogatif se place en début de phrase.

On utilise le radical du verbe principal.

🔊

19.9 CONSTRUCTION LES QUESTIONS OUVERTES AVEC « DO » ET « DOES »

MOT INTERROGATIF	DO/DOES	SUJET	VERBE + COMPLÉMENT
When	do	I / you / we / they	eat lunch?
	does	he / she / it	

19.10 AUTRES EXEMPLES LES QUESTIONS OUVERTES AVEC « DO » ET « DOES »

Where do **you go swimming?**

When does **he finish work?**

What does **she do on the weekend?**

Which **car** do **you drive to work?**

🔊

19.11 COMPLÉTEZ LES QUESTIONS.

When ____*do*____ they start work?

❶ When _____ she eat lunch?

❷ Where _____ they live?

❸ Which bag _____ you want?

❹ Where _____ he come from?

❺ When _____ the movie end?

🔊

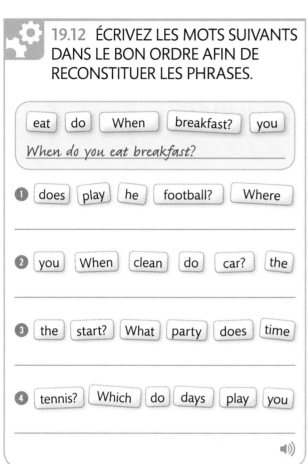

19.12 ÉCRIVEZ LES MOTS SUIVANTS DANS LE BON ORDRE AFIN DE RECONSTITUER LES PHRASES.

eat | do | When | breakfast? | you

When do you eat breakfast?

❶ does | play | he | football? | Where

_____

❷ you | When | clean | do | car? | the

_____

❸ the | start? | What | party | does | time

_____

❹ tennis? | Which | do | days | play | you

_____

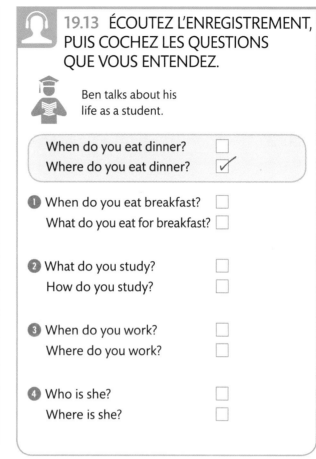

19.13 ÉCOUTEZ L'ENREGISTREMENT, PUIS COCHEZ LES QUESTIONS QUE VOUS ENTENDEZ.

Ben talks about his life as a student.

When do you eat dinner? ☐
Where do you eat dinner? ☑

❶ When do you eat breakfast? ☐
What do you eat for breakfast? ☐

❷ What do you study? ☐
How do you study? ☐

❸ When do you work? ☐
Where do you work? ☐

❹ Who is she? ☐
Where is she? ☐

19.14 COMPLÉTEZ LES PHRASES, PUIS LISEZ-LES À VOIX HAUTE.

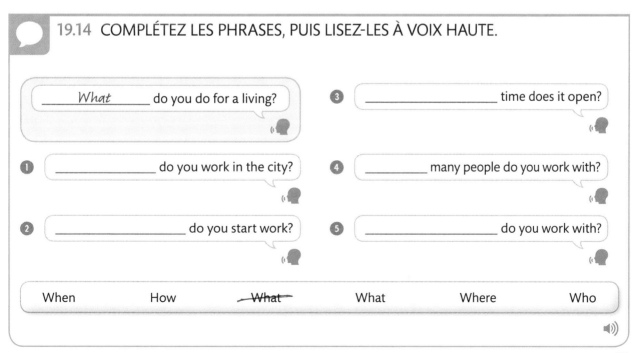

___*What*___ do you do for a living?

❶ _____ do you work in the city?

❷ _____ do you start work?

❸ _____ time does it open?

❹ _____ many people do you work with?

❺ _____ do you work with?

When | How | ~~What~~ | What | Where | Who

19.15 LISEZ LE COURRIEL, PUIS RÉPONDEZ AUX QUESTIONS.

Which village is Bernadette in?
Torremolinos ☐
Mijas ☑

To: Mary Jones

Subject: Vacation in Spain

Hi Mary.

We're in Spain, in a village called Mijas, near Torremolinos. My sister is at work this week, so I'm here with my brother, John. Our hotel is next to some apartments. It's in a complex and has two swimming pools and a gym. Breakfast is from 7:30am until 9 every morning, so I get up at 7am and have a swim before I eat. John stays in his room and we meet later for breakfast. The restaurant is by the pool. We have our breakfast there every day. There's also dancing at night. There's salsa dancing tonight, and tomorrow it's flamenco.

See you soon,
Bernadette

① Who is Bernadette on vacation with?
Her brother ☐
Her sister ☐

② How many swimming pools does the hotel have?
Two ☐
Three ☐

③ What time does Bernadette get up?
At 7am ☐
At 7:30am ☐

④ What does Bernadette do in the morning?
Goes to the gym ☐
Goes swimming ☐

⑤ Where does Bernadette have breakfast?
In her room ☐
By the pool ☐

⑥ When is the flamenco dancing?
Tonight ☐
Tomorrow ☐

19.16 UTILISEZ LE SCHÉMA POUR CRÉER 12 PHRASES, PUIS LISEZ-LES À VOIX HAUTE.

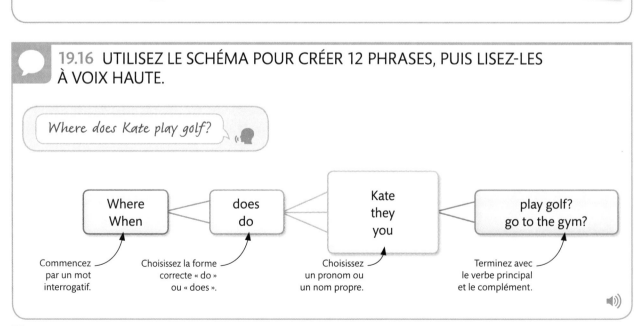

Where does Kate play golf?

| Where / When | does / do | Kate / they / you | play golf? / go to the gym? |

Commencez par un mot interrogatif.

Choisissez la forme correcte « do » ou « does ».

Choisissez un pronom ou un nom propre.

Terminez avec le verbe principal et le complément.

> Where are my laptop?
> _Where is my laptop?_

❶ How often does they play tennis?

_____

❷ Which office do he work in?

_____

❸ Where are the party?

_____

❹ What does you do?

_____

🔊

> When _does Russell go to the gym?_
> Russell goes to the gym on Tuesdays.

❶ What _____ ?

Her cat is called Ginger.

❷ Who _____ ?

My English teacher is Mrs. Price.

❸ Where _____ ?

Ben works in a hospital.

❹ How _____ ?

My grandmother is fine, thanks.

🔊

19 ✓ CHECK-LIST

⚙ Les questions ouvertes ☐   **Aa** Les mots interrogatifs ☐   🧩 Demander des précisions ☐

🔄 **BILAN** L'ANGLAIS QUE VOUS AVEZ APPRIS DANS LES CHAPITRES 15-19

NOUVEAU POINT LINGUISTIQUE	EXEMPLE TYPE	☑	CHAPITRE
LA FORME NÉGATIVE AVEC « TO BE »	**I am a farmer.** I am not **a doctor.** **You're not a doctor. You aren't a doctor.**	☐	15.1, 15.3, 15.7
LA FORME NÉGATIVE DU PRÉSENT SIMPLE	**He** does not work **inside. He** works **outside.** **I** work **outside. I** do not work **inside.**	☐	16.1, 16.3, 16.6
LES QUESTIONS SIMPLES	**Are you Canadian? Do you work in an office?** **Does she work in a school?**	☐	17.1, 17.8
LES RÉPONSES COURTES	**Are you a doctor?** Yes, I am. **Do you work in an office?** No, I don't.	☐	18.1, 18.2
LES QUESTIONS OUVERTES AVEC « TO BE »	**My name is Sarah.** What **is your name?**	☐	19.1, 19.2
LES QUESTIONS OUVERTES AVEC « DO » ET « DOES »	When do **you eat lunch?** When does **she eat lunch?**	☐	19.8, 19.9

20.1 EN VILLE

village

town

city

hospital

police station

bus station

bus stop

train station

airport

school

factory

supermarket

store (US)
shop (UK)

pharmacy

bank

post office

library

museum

town hall

castle

office building

park

here

bridge

swimming pool

restaurant

café

there

bar

movie theater (US)
cinema (UK)

theater (US)
theatre (UK)

hotel

near

church

mosque

synagogue

temple

far

21 Parler de votre ville

Lorsque vous parlez de la présence de quelque chose, vous pouvez utiliser « there is » pour une chose et « there are » pour plusieurs. Les formes négatives sont « there isn't » et « there aren't ».

🔧 **Grammaire** « There is » et « there are »
Aa Vocabulaire Les villes et les bâtiments
🧩 **Compétence** Décrire une ville

21.1 POINT CLÉ « THERE IS » ET « THERE ARE »

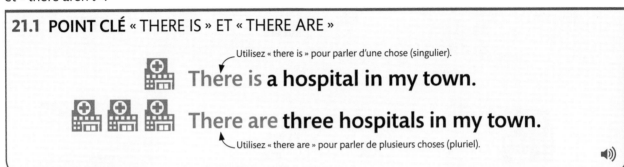

Utilisez « there is » pour parler d'une chose (singulier).

There is **a hospital in my town.**

There are **three hospitals in my town.**

Utilisez « there are » pour parler de plusieurs choses (pluriel).

21.2 AUTRES EXEMPLES « THERE IS » ET « THERE ARE »

There is **an airport.**

There are **two theaters.**

There is **a hotel.**

There are **three cafés.**

21.3 COMPLÉTEZ LES PHRASES AVEC « THERE IS » OU « THERE ARE ».

There is a factory.

❶ _____ two churches.

❷ _____ a swimming pool.

❸ _____ a library.

❹ _____ two castles.

21.4 PRONONCEZ CES FORMES DU PLURIEL À VOIX HAUTE.

libraries 🗣

❶ airports 🗣   ❺ bars 🗣

❷ theaters 🗣   ❻ churches 🗣

❸ schools 🗣   ❼ factories 🗣

❹ hospitals 🗣   ❽ offices 🗣

21.5 OBSERVEZ LES IMAGES, PUIS COMPLÉTEZ LES PHRASES.

There is a ___town hall___ .

❶ There are _____ .

❷ There are _____ .

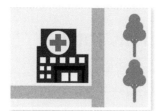

❸ There is a _____ .

❹ There is a _____ .

❺ There are _____ .

21.6 POINT CLÉ « THERE IS NOT » ET « THERE ARE NOT ANY »

Ajoutez « not » pour former
une phrase négative au singulier.

There is **not a school.**

There isn't **a school.**

Vous pouvez utiliser
la forme contractée de
« is not » : « isn't ».

Ajoutez « not any » pour former
une phrase négative au pluriel.

There are **not any schools.**

There aren't **any schools.**

Vous pouvez utiliser la forme
contractée de « are not » :
« aren't ».

21.7 BARREZ LE MOT INCORRECT DANS CHAQUE PHRASE.

There isn't / ~~aren't~~ a castle.

❶ There isn't / aren't a theater.

❷ There isn't / aren't any factories.

❸ There isn't / aren't a bus station.

❹ There isn't / aren't any airports.

❺ There isn't / aren't any churches.

21.8 DIRE AUTREMENT
« THERE AREN'T ANY »

Vous pouvez utiliser « are no » au lieu de « aren't any ».
Les 2 formes veulent dire la même chose.

Ceci est la forme contractée
de « are not ».

There aren't any stores.

There are no stores.
🔊

21.9 AUTRES EXEMPLES « ARE NO »

There are no **libraries in Oldtown.**

There are no **factories in Newport.**

There are no **schools in our village.**
🔊

21.10 COMPLÉTEZ LES PHRASES AVEC « ARE » OU « AREN'T ».

> There _____*aren't*_____ any theaters.

1. There _____ no castles.

2. There _____ any factories.

3. There _____ no hospitals.

4. There _____ any churches.

5. There _____ no swimming pools.

6. There _____ no airports.
🔊

21.11 ÉCOUTEZ L'ENREGISTREMENT, PUIS NUMÉROTEZ LES IMAGES DANS LE BON ORDRE.

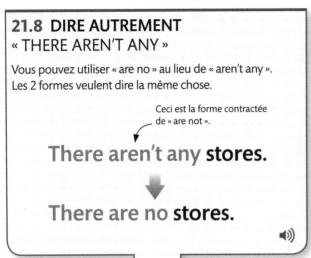

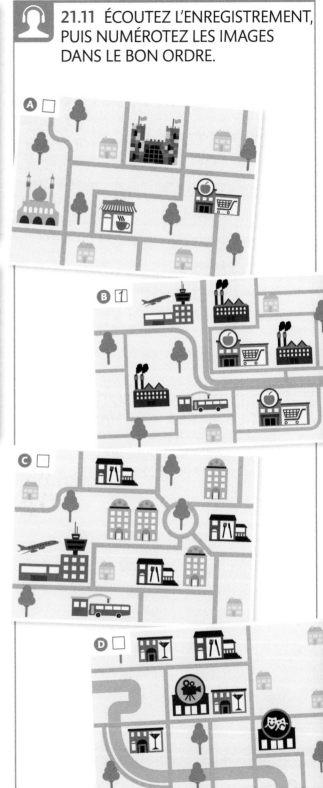

21.12 LISEZ LE COURRIEL, PUIS COCHEZ LES BONNES RÉPONSES.

There are two schools.
True ☐ **False** ☑

1 There is a supermarket.

True ☐ **False** ☐

2 There is a theater.

True ☐ **False** ☐

3 There are four movie theaters.

True ☐ **False** ☐

4 There are three restaurants.

True ☐ **False** ☐

✉

To: Matt

Subject: Our new place

Hi Matt,

We're in our new house in Littleton and it's great! There are three schools in the town, so that's good for the children. There's also a big swimming pool and Joanne goes there every evening. I work in an office above the supermarket. It's near our house.

There are lots of things to do on the weekend. There isn't a theater, but there are two movie theaters, three restaurants, and a library. There's also a great museum. We go there every weekend because the children love it!

Come and see us soon. It's easy to get here. There isn't an airport or a train station, but there's a bus station.

See you soon! Jamal

↩ ↩↩

21.13 OBSERVEZ L'IMAGE, PUIS COMPLÉTEZ LES PHRASES ET LISEZ-LES À VOIX HAUTE.

There is a supermarket.

1 _____ a park.

2 _____ a hotel.

3 _____ no cafés.

4 _____ an airport.

5 _____ stores.

6 _____ a train station.

7 _____ theaters.

---

21 ✔ CHECK-LIST

⚙ « There is » et « there are » ☐   **Aa** Les villes et les bâtiments ☐   🧩 Décrire une ville ☐

22 « A » et « the »

Utilisez l'article défini (« the ») ou indéfini (« a », « an »)
pour parler de choses de manière spécifique ou générale.
Utilisez « some » pour parler de plusieurs choses.

⚙ **Grammaire** Les articles définis et indéfinis
Aa Vocabulaire Les lieux dans la ville
🧩 **Compétence** Les articles

22.1 POINT CLÉ « A », « AN » ET « THE »

Utilisez « a » pour
parler de quelque
chose en général.
Utilisez « the » pour
parler d'un endroit,
d'une personne
ou d'une chose que
votre interlocuteur
et vous-même
connaissez.

Utilisez « a » parce que vous parlez de votre travail
en général, et non pas du lieu exact où vous travaillez.

I work in a library.

I work in the library on Main Street.

Utilisez « the » parce que vous parlez spécifiquement
du bâtiment dans lequel vous travaillez.

🔊

22.2 AUTRES EXEMPLES « A », « AN » ET « THE »

Utilisez « a/an » pour parler
de métiers.

Jim is an artist.

Utilisez « an » devant les mots
commençant par une voyelle.

Is there a bank near here?

Utilisez « a » avec « is
there » et « there is ».

Utilisez « the » pour parler d'un médecin
en particulier.

The doctor at my hospital is good.

I go to the bank on Broad Street.

Utilisez « the » pour parler d'une banque
précise.

🔊

22.3 BARREZ LE MOT INCORRECT DANS CHAQUE PHRASE.

Charlotte is ~~a~~ / an / ~~the~~ actress.

1. A / An / The new teacher is called Miss Jones.

2. There is a / an / the good café in the park.

3. I work at a / an / the hotel next to the library.

4. There is a / an / the swimming pool near my office.

5. It is a / an / the dog's favorite toy.

6. Janie is a / an / the artist at the gallery.

7. See you at a / an / the café at the bus station.

 🔊

22.4 POINT CLÉ « A » ET « SOME »

"A" et "an" ne s'utilisent qu'avec des noms singuliers. On utilise « some » avec des noms pluriels.

Utilisez « a » et « an » pour parler d'une seule chose.

Singulier.

There is a hotel in the town.

There are some hotels in the town.

Utilisez « some » pour parler de plusieurs choses.

Pluriel.

22.5 AUTRES EXEMPLES « A » ET « SOME »

There is a bank on Main Street.

There are some banks on Main Street.

There is a waiter over there.

There are some children in the park.

22.6 COMPLÉTEZ LES PHRASES AVEC « A » OU « SOME ».

There is ____a____ restaurant in the park.

1 There are _____ stores on Broad Street.

2 There is _____ café next to the castle.

3 There are _____ cakes on the table.

4 There is _____ phone here.

5 There are _____ factories downtown.

22.7 RÉCRIVEZ LES PHRASES EN CORRIGEANT LES ERREURS.

There **are** a movie theater on Main Street.
There is a movie theater on Main Street.

1 There **is** some supermarkets in town.

_____

2 There **are** an office near the river.

_____

3 There **is** some chocolate bars in my bag.

_____

4 There **are** a hospital near the bus station.

_____

22.8 POINT CLÉ LES QUESTIONS AVEC « A » ET « ANY »

There is a hotel in the town.

Is there a hotel in the town?

Utilisez « a » pour demander
s'il y a une chose.

There are some hotels in the town.

Are there any hotels in the town?

Utilisez « any » pour demander
s'il y a plusieurs choses.

22.9 AUTRES EXEMPLES LES QUESTIONS AVEC « A » ET « ANY »

Is there a restaurant?

Is there a hospital?

Are there any factories?

Are there any theaters?

22.10 BARREZ LES MOTS INCORRECTS DANS CHAQUE PHRASE.

Is there a / ~~an~~ / ~~any~~ hospital in the town?

1 Are there a / an / any stores on your street?

2 Is there a / an / any airport near Littleton?

3 Are there a / an / any mosques in the city?

4 Is there a / an / any swimming pool downtown?

5 Are there a / an / any offices in that building?

22.11 ÉCRIVEZ LES MOTS SUIVANTS DANS LE BON ORDRE AFIN DE RECONSTITUER LES PHRASES.

any | in | town? | Are | your | factories | there

Are there any factories in your town?

1 there | here? | a | Is | supermarket | near

2 on | there | any | Elm Road? | Are | cafés

3 Are | your house? | there | any | near | hotels

4 a | café | office? | there | near | Is | your

5 the | there | a bar | next to | Is | bank?

22.12 POINT CLÉ LES RÉPONSES COURTES

Lorsque vous répondez à une question en anglais, vous n'êtes pas obligé de répéter tous les mots de la question.

Forme réduite de « Yes, there is a hotel in the town ».

Is there a hotel in the town?

Yes, there is.

No, there isn't.

Are there any hotels in the town?

Yes, there are.

No, there aren't.

Forme réduite de « No, there aren't any hotels in the town ».

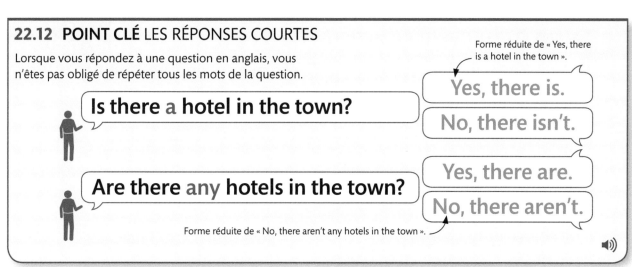

22.13 COMPLÉTEZ LES PHRASES AVEC UNE RÉPONSE COURTE.

Are there any theaters in Littleton?
No, *there aren't* .

1. Is there a church on Main Street?
Yes, _____.

2. Are there any pens in your bag?
Yes, _____.

3. Is there a post office near here?
No, _____.

4. Are there any supermarkets on Station Road?
Yes, _____.

5. Is there a school near your house?
No, _____.

6. Are there any dogs in the hotel?
No, _____.

22.14 ÉTUDIEZ LA CARTE, RÉPONDEZ AUX QUESTIONS, PUIS LISEZ LES PHRASES À VOIX HAUTE.

Is there a library?   *Yes, there is.*

1. Are there any hotels?

2. Is there a church?

3. Are there two cafés?

4. Is there a supermarket?

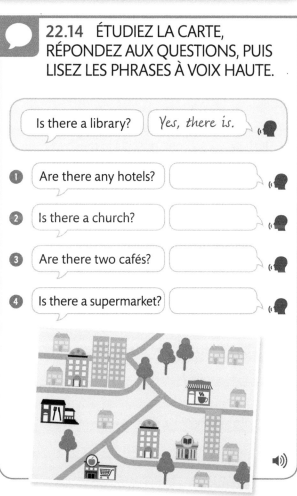

Utilisez l'impératif pour ordonner à quelqu'un de faire quelque chose. L'impératif permet également d'avertir une personne d'un danger ou de lui indiquer une direction.

⚙ **Grammaire** L'impératif
Aa Vocabulaire Les directions
🧩 **Compétence** Trouver votre chemin

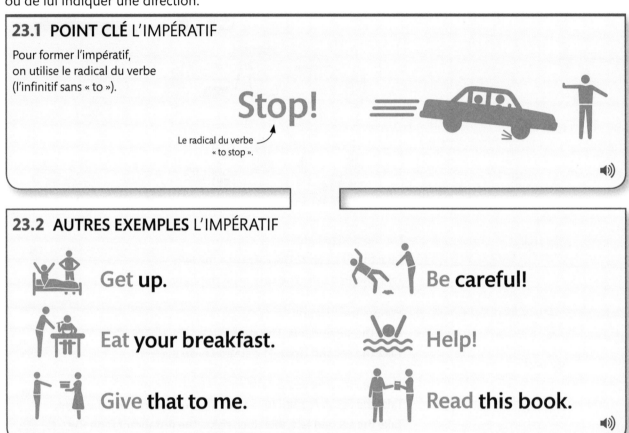

23.1 POINT CLÉ L'IMPÉRATIF

Pour former l'impératif,
on utilise le radical du verbe
(l'infinitif sans « to »).

Stop!

Le radical du verbe
« to stop ».

23.2 AUTRES EXEMPLES L'IMPÉRATIF

Get up.

Eat your breakfast.

Give that to me.

Be careful!

Help!

Read this book.

23.3 TRANSFORMEZ LES INFINITIFS EN IMPÉRATIFS.

| to go | = | *Go* |

1 to wake up = _____
2 to do = _____
3 to start = _____

4 to have = _____
5 to wait = _____
6 to stop = _____
7 to work = _____

23.4 POINT CLÉ
DONNER UNE DIRECTION

↑ go straight ahead

....

↰ turn left

....

↱ turn right

....

go past

....

take the first right

....

take the second right

....

🔊

23.5 COCHEZ LES DIRECTIONS QUI VOUS MÈNENT AU BON ENDROIT SUR LA CARTE.

For the Bridge Café:
Take the first right. The café is on the left. ☑
Take the first left. The café is on the right. ☐

❶ For the train station:
Take the second left. The station is on the right. ☐
Take the second right. The station is on the left. ☐

❷ For the Elm Tree Restaurant:
Take the first left, then turn right. The restaurant is on the right. ☐
Take the second left, then turn right. The restaurant is on the left. ☐

❸ For the hospital:
Take the second right, and the hospital is on the left. ☐
Take the second left, and the hospital is on the right. ☐

❹ For the Supreme Hotel:
Take the first left, then go straight ahead. The hotel is on the right. ☐
Take the first right, then go straight ahead. The hotel is on the left. ☐

❺ For the castle:
Take the first left, then turn right. The castle is on the left. ☐
Take the first left, then turn left. The castle is on the right. ☐

🔊

23.6 VOCABULAIRE LES DIRECTIONS

next to

....

opposite

....

between

....

on the corner

....

behind

....

in front of

....

on the right

....

on the left

....

**intersection (US)
crossroads (UK)**

....

block

....

🔊

Aa ## 23.7 COMPLÉTEZ LES PHRASES AVEC LES DIRECTIONS APPROPRIÉES.

The Rathbone Theater is
____*opposite*____the park.

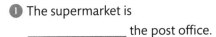

❶ The supermarket is
_____ the post office.

❷ The museum is
_____ the café.

❸ The station is
_____ the church.

❹ The cinema is on the
_____of the intersection.

❺ The post office is_____
the café and the supermarket.

 🔊

23.8 POINT CLÉ L'IMPÉRATIF NÉGATIF

Ajoutez « don't »
ou « do not » devant
le verbe pour former
l'impératif négatif.

Do not
Don't } turn **right.**

🔊

23.9 AUTRES EXEMPLES L'IMPÉRATIF NÉGATIF

Don't eat **that cake.**

Don't sit **there.**

🔊

 ## 23.10 TRANSFORMEZ LES PHRASES À LA FORME NÉGATIVE.

Take the first left.
Don't take the first left.

❶ Read that book.

_____

❷ Go past the hotel.

_____

❸ Give that to the cat.

_____

❹ Have a shower.

_____

❺ Drive to the mall.

_____

🔊

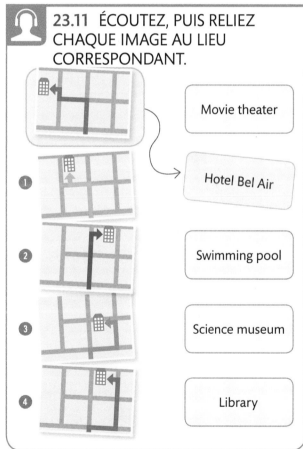

23.11 ÉCOUTEZ, PUIS RELIEZ CHAQUE IMAGE AU LIEU CORRESPONDANT.

Movie theater

Hotel Bel Air

Swimming pool

Science museum

Library

24 Relier les phrases

« And » et « but » sont des conjonctions : des mots qui relient des phrases. « And » permet d'ajouter des éléments à une phrase ou de relier des phrases. « But » introduit un contraste.

⚙ Grammaire « And » et « but »
Aa Vocabulaire La ville, les métiers et la famille
🧩 Compétence Relier les phrases

24.1 POINT CLÉ « AND » POUR RELIER DES PHRASES

Utilisez « and » pour relier deux phrases.

« There's » est identique à « there is ».

There's a library. There's a restaurant.

There's a library and a restaurant.

Vous pouvez omettre le second « there's » lorsque vous reliez les phrases avec « and ».

🔊

24.2 AUTRES EXEMPLES « AND » POUR RELIER DES PHRASES

 Jazmin's sister lives and works in Paris.

 My father and brother are both engineers.

 Simon plays video games and watches TV every night.

🔊

 ## 24.3 RELIEZ LES PHRASES SUIVANTES AVEC « AND ».

I get up. I have a shower.
I get up and have a shower.

❶ There are two hotels. There are three shops.
_____

❷ Hilda works in a school. She works in a theater.
_____

❸ My uncle is a scientist. My aunt is a doctor.
_____

❹ Sue watches TV. She reads books.
_____

❺ The store opens at night. Jan starts work.
_____

🔊

24.4 ÉCOUTEZ, PUIS RELIEZ LES LIEUX MENTIONNÉS AVEC « AND ».

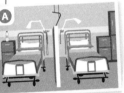

24.5 POINT CLÉ UTILISER UNE VIRGULE AU LIEU DE « AND »

Pour les listes de deux éléments ou plus, vous pouvez utiliser la virgule au lieu de « and ».

Vous pouvez utiliser une virgule pour remplacer « and » dans une liste.

Utilisez une autre virgule devant le « and ».

There's a library, a store, and a café.

Conservez le « and » entre les deux derniers noms.

24.6 COCHEZ LES PHRASES DANS LESQUELLES LES VIRGULES ET « AND » SONT UTILISÉS CORRECTEMENT.

I am a wife, a mother, and a daughter. ☑
I am a wife, and a mother, a daughter. ☐

❶ There are hotels and bars and stores. ☐
There are hotels, bars, and stores. ☐

❷ Sam eats, breakfast lunch and dinner. ☐
Sam eats breakfast, lunch, and dinner. ☐

❸ I play tennis, soccer, and chess. ☐
I play tennis, and soccer, and chess. ☐

❹ Teo plays with his car and his train and his bus. ☐
Teo plays with his car, train, and bus. ☐

❺ There is a pencil, a bag and, a cell phone. ☐
There is a pencil, a bag, and a cell phone. ☐

❻ My friends, girlfriend, and aunt are here. ☐
My friends, and, girlfriend and aunt are here. ☐

❼ Ling works on Monday, Thursday, and Friday. ☐
Ling works on Monday, and Thursday, Friday. ☐

24.7 POINT CLÉ « BUT » POUR RELIER DES PHRASES

Utilisez « but » pour relier une phrase affirmative et une phrase négative.

There's a hotel. There isn't a store.

There's a hotel, but there isn't a store.

Vous pouvez utiliser « but » pour ajouter un élément négatif à une phrase affirmative.

There isn't a store here, but there is a hotel.

Vous pouvez utiliser « but » pour ajouter un élément affirmatif à une phrase négative.

24.8 RELIEZ CHAQUE DÉBUT DE PHRASE À LA FIN CORRESPONDANTE.

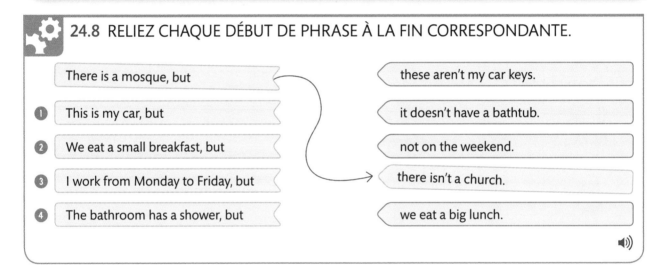

There is a mosque, but — there isn't a church.

① This is my car, but — these aren't my car keys.

② We eat a small breakfast, but — it doesn't have a bathtub.

③ I work from Monday to Friday, but — not on the weekend.

④ The bathroom has a shower, but — we eat a big lunch.

24.9 RELIEZ LES PHRASES SUIVANTES AVEC « BUT ».

There is a post office. There isn't a bank.
There is a post office, but there isn't a bank.

① There isn't a bathtub. There is a shower.

_____

② There isn't a bar. There is a café.

_____

③ This bag is Maya's. That laptop isn't hers.

_____

④ Si doesn't have any dogs. He has two cats.

_____

⑤ Sally reads books. She never watches TV.

_____

24.10 BARREZ LE MOT INCORRECT DANS CHAQUE PHRASE.

I am a father and / ~~but~~ a son.

❶ Lu reads books and / but magazines.

❷ I work every weekday, and / but not on weekends.

❸ Jim is a husband and / but a father.

❹ There is a cinema, and / but no theater.

❺ There isn't a gym, and / but there is a pool.

🔊

24.11 ÉCRIVEZ DES PHRASES AVEC « AND » ET « BUT » D'APRÈS LES IMAGES DU TABLEAU, PUIS LISEZ-LES À VOIX HAUTE.

There is _____a mosque and a church,_____
_____but there isn't a factory_____ .

❶ There is _____
_____ .

❷ There is _____
_____ .

❸ There is _____
_____ .

❹ There is _____
_____ .

🔊

Utilisez des adjectifs pour donner des informations supplémentaires sur un nom ; pour décrire une personne, un bâtiment ou un lieu, par exemple.

⚙ **Grammaire** Les adjectifs

Aa Vocabulaire Les adjectifs et les noms de lieux

🧩 **Compétence** Décrire des lieux

25.1 POINT CLÉ LES ADJECTIFS

Les adjectifs se placent généralement devant le nom qu'ils décrivent.

She is a busy woman.

He is a busy man.

Les adjectifs sont les mêmes, que le nom soit masculin ou féminin.

It is a busy town.

These are busy streets.

Les adjectifs sont les mêmes, que le nom soit au singulier ou au pluriel.

25.2 VOCABULAIRE LES ADJECTIFS

old

new

beautiful

horrible

busy

quiet

small

big

25.3 ÉCRIVEZ LES MOTS SUIVANTS DANS LE BON ORDRE AFIN DE RECONSTITUER LES PHRASES.

a | This | is | town. | beautiful

This is a beautiful town.

1 horrible | is | He | man. | a

_____

2 are | They | small | children.

_____

3 uncle | My | man. | is | a quiet

_____

4 large | is | There | a | cake.

_____

5 my | shoes. | are | old | These

_____

6 supermarket. | a | new | is | There

_____

7 in | work | You | museum. | an old

_____

🔊

25.4 AUTRES EMPLOIS LES ADJECTIFS

Les adjectifs peuvent parfois se placer à d'autres endroits dans la phrase.

The town is busy.

Vous pouvez placer l'adjectif à la fin de la phrase après le verbe « to be ».

Southbay is a busy town.

L'adjectif se place généralement devant le nom.

It is busy.

Vous pouvez remplacer le nom par un pronom.

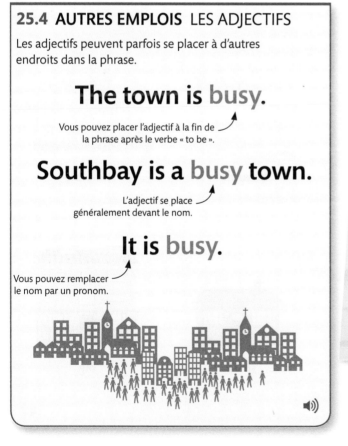

🔊

Aa 25.5 LISEZ LE TEXTE ET ENTOUREZ 7 ADJECTIFS.

Hi! I'm Paolo.

I live and work in a (small) town.
There are some beautiful old buildings
there and lots of hotels, too. I work
in a large restaurant near the river.
I'm a waiter and my friend is the chef.
The restaurant is busy every evening
and my job is horrible, but the food
is beautiful. I eat there every day.

25.6 RÉCRIVEZ LA PHRASE DE 2 MANIÈRES DIFFÉRENTES.

Rome is an old city.	The city is old.	It is old.
① She is a busy nurse.		
② He is a quiet dog.		
③ They are new patients.		
④ It is a horrible town.		
⑤ It is a beautiful car.		

25.7 VOCABULAIRE LES LIEUX ET LES PAYSAGES

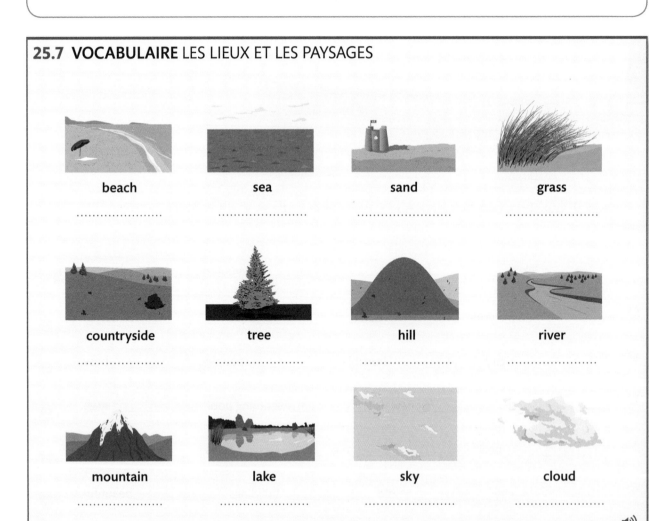

beach ....

sea ....

sand ....

grass ....

countryside ....

tree ....

hill ....

river ....

mountain ....

lake ....

sky ....

cloud ....

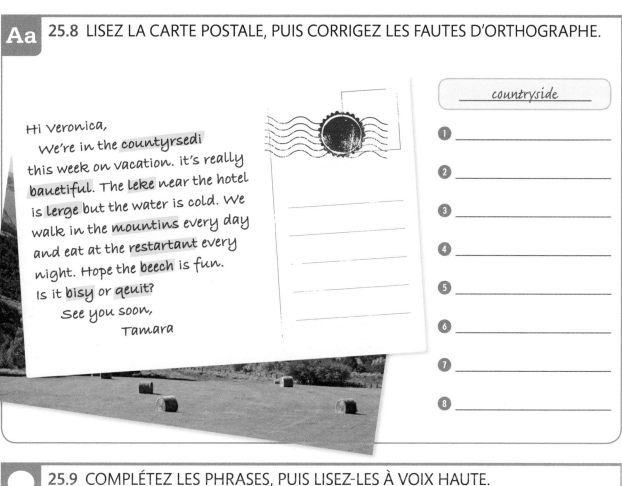

Aa 25.8 LISEZ LA CARTE POSTALE, PUIS CORRIGEZ LES FAUTES D'ORTHOGRAPHE.

Hi Veronica,
 We're in the countyrsedi this week on vacation. it's really bauetiful. The leke near the hotel is lerge but the water is cold. We walk in the mountins every day and eat at the restartant every night. Hope the beech is fun.
Is it bisy or qeuit?
 See you soon,
 Tamara

countryside

1 _____

2 _____

3 _____

4 _____

5 _____

6 _____

7 _____

8 _____

25.9 COMPLÉTEZ LES PHRASES, PUIS LISEZ-LES À VOIX HAUTE.

_____The_____ lakes _____are_____ beautiful _____and the_____ mountain _____is_____ large.

1 _____ countryside _____ quiet _____ trees _____ beautiful.

2 _____ city _____ horrible _____ people _____ busy.

3 _____ hotel _____ new _____ swimming pool _____ large.

4 _____ beach _____ big _____ cafés _____ busy.

5 _____ city _____ old _____ buildings _____ beautiful.

25.10 POINT CLÉ LES EXPRESSIONS DE QUANTITÉ

La langue anglaise dispose de nombreuses expressions pour parler de quantités approximatives.

Utilisez « some » lorsqu'il y a plus d'un élément mais lorsque l'on ne sait pas exactement combien.

There are some buildings.

Utilisez « a few » pour une faible quantité.

There are a few buildings.

Utilisez « lots of » pour une grande quantité.

There are lots of buildings.

25.11 AUTRES EXEMPLES LES EXPRESSIONS DE QUANTITÉ

There are some trees.

There are lots of people.

There are lots of mountains.

There are a few cars.

25.12 ÉCOUTEZ L'ENREGISTREMENT, PUIS NUMÉROTEZ LES IMAGES DANS LE BON ORDRE.

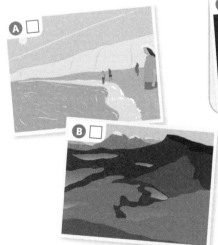

25.13 RÉDIGEZ 4 PHRASES POUR DÉCRIRE L'IMAGE AVEC « A FEW », « SOME » OU « LOTS OF ».

_____There are some_____ trees.

❶ _____ people.

❷ _____ buildings.

❸ _____ cars.

❹ _____ parks.

25.14 OBSERVEZ LE TABLEAU, ÉCRIVEZ DES PHRASES AVEC « A FEW », « SOME » ET « LOTS OF », PUIS LISEZ-LES À VOIX HAUTE.

	A FEW	SOME	LOTS OF
In Greenpoint,	🏠		🚶
❶ In the tree,	🐦	🍎	
❷ In the sea,	🚶		🐟
❸ In the countryside,		🚶	🌳

In Greenpoint, there are
a few buildings and lots of people.

25 ✓ CHECK-LIST

⚙ Les adjectifs ☐   **Aa** Les adjectifs et les noms de lieux ☐   🧩 Décrire des lieux ☐

26 Donner des raisons

Utilisez la conjonction « because » pour donner une raison. Vous pouvez aussi utiliser « because » pour répondre à la question « Why? ».

⚙ **Grammaire** « Because »
Aa Vocabulaire Les lieux et les métiers
🧩 **Compétence** Donner des raisons

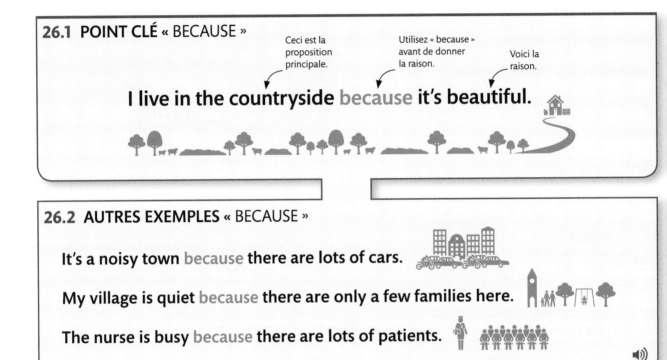

26.1 POINT CLÉ « BECAUSE »

Ceci est la proposition principale.

Utilisez « because » avant de donner la raison.

Voici la raison.

I live in the countryside because it's beautiful.

26.2 AUTRES EXEMPLES « BECAUSE »

It's a noisy town because there are lots of cars.

My village is quiet because there are only a few families here.

The nurse is busy because there are lots of patients.

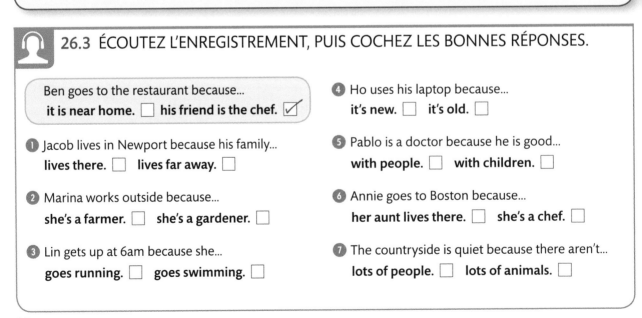

26.3 ÉCOUTEZ L'ENREGISTREMENT, PUIS COCHEZ LES BONNES RÉPONSES.

Ben goes to the restaurant because...
it is near home. ☐ **his friend is the chef.** ☑

❶ Jacob lives in Newport because his family...
lives there. ☐ **lives far away.** ☐

❷ Marina works outside because...
she's a farmer. ☐ **she's a gardener.** ☐

❸ Lin gets up at 6am because she...
goes running. ☐ **goes swimming.** ☐

❹ Ho uses his laptop because...
it's new. ☐ **it's old.** ☐

❺ Pablo is a doctor because he is good...
with people. ☐ **with children.** ☐

❻ Annie goes to Boston because...
her aunt lives there. ☐ **she's a chef.** ☐

❼ The countryside is quiet because there aren't...
lots of people. ☐ **lots of animals.** ☐

26.4 COMPLÉTEZ LES PHRASES AVEC CELLES DE LA LISTE.

I work in a theater because ___*I'm an actor*___ .

1 She lives on a farm because _____ .

2 She works in a hotel because _____ .

3 They get up late because _____ .

4 We work with children because _____ .

5 You don't eat lunch because _____ .

6 I work outside because _____ .

7 My parents go to the countryside because _____ .

I'm a gardener

we're teachers

~~I'm an actor~~

you're busy

she's a farmer

they're students

it's quiet

she's a receptionist

◀))

---

26 ✓ CHECK-LIST

⚙ « Because » ☐   **Aa** Les lieux et les métiers ☐   🧩 Donner des raisons ☐

♻ BILAN L'ANGLAIS QUE VOUS AVEZ APPRIS DANS LES CHAPITRES 21-26

NOUVEAU POINT LINGUISTIQUE	EXEMPLE TYPE	☑	CHAPITRE
« THERE IS » ET « THERE ARE »	There is **a hospital.** There are **three hospitals.** There isn't **a school.** There aren't any **schools.**	☐	21.1, 21.6
LES ARTICLES	I **work in** a library. I **work in** the library **on Main Street.**	☐	22.1
« ANY » ET « SOME »	**Are there** any **hotels? There are** some **hotels.**	☐	22.8
L'IMPÉRATIF	Stop! Be **careful!**	☐	23.1
RELIER LES PHRASES	**There's a library** and **a restaurant.** **There's a hotel,** but **there isn't a store.**	☐	24.1, 24.7
LES ADJECTIFS	**She is a** busy **woman. It is a** busy **town.** **The town is** busy. **It is** busy.	☐	25.1, 25.4
« BECAUSE »	**I live in the countryside** because **it's beautiful.**	☐	26.1

27 Vocabulaire

27.1 DANS LA MAISON

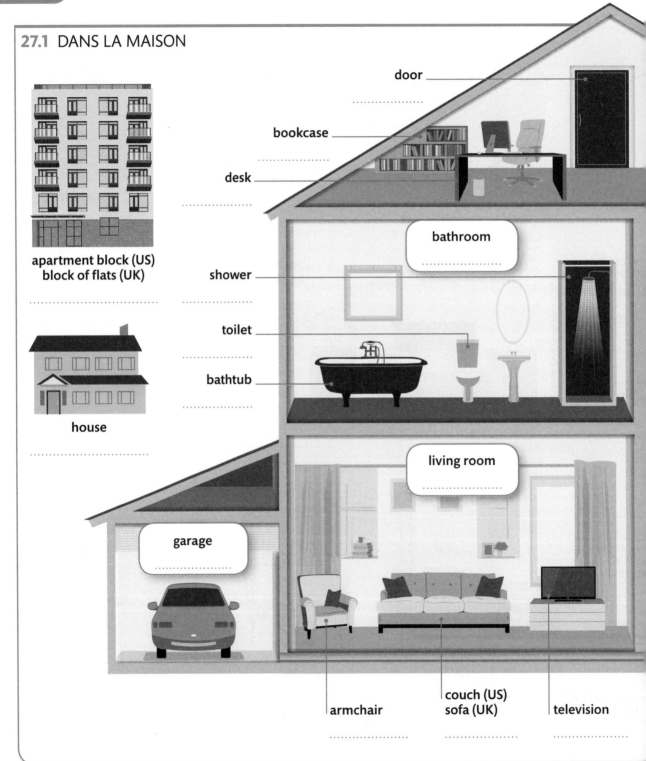

apartment block (US)
block of flats (UK)

house

door

bookcase

desk

bathroom

shower

toilet

bathtub

living room

garage

armchair

couch (US)
sofa (UK)

television

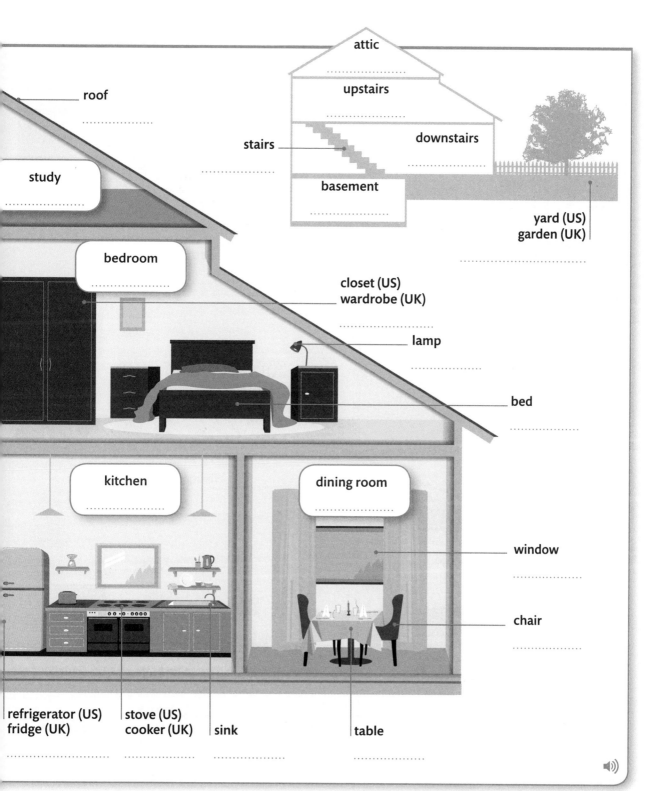

attic

upstairs

roof

stairs

downstairs

study

basement

yard (US)
garden (UK)

bedroom

closet (US)
wardrobe (UK)

lamp

bed

kitchen

dining room

window

chair

refrigerator (US)
fridge (UK)

stove (US)
cooker (UK)

sink

table

28 Ce que vous possédez

Vous pouvez utiliser le verbe « to have » lorsque vous parlez de choses que vous possédez, telles que des meubles ou des animaux domestiques. Vous pouvez également employer ce verbe pour parler de vos diplômes, d'appareils électroménagers ou des pièces de votre maison.

🔧 **Grammaire** « Have »
Aa Vocabulaire Les objets dans la maison
🧩 **Compétence** Parler de ce que vous possédez

28.1 POINT CLÉ « TO HAVE »

« To have » est un verbe irrégulier. La troisième personne du singulier est « has », et non pas « have ».

Utilisez « has » pour la troisième personne du singulier (« he », « she » ou « it »).

I have a garage.

She has a yard.

28.2 CONSTRUCTION LES PHRASES AFFIRMATIVES AVEC « HAVE »

Après ces pronoms, on utilise « have ».

Après ces pronoms, on utilise « has ».

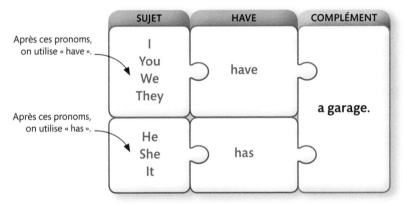

SUJET	HAVE	COMPLÉMENT
I You We They	have	a garage.
He She It	has	

28.3 COMPLÉTEZ LES PHRASES AVEC « HAVE » OU « HAS ».

 I _____*have*_____ a house.

 ❶ They _____ a car.

❷ You _____ a chair.

 ❸ He _____ a dog.

 ❹ We _____ a daughter.

 ❺ It _____ a door.

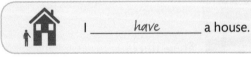

102

28.4 ÉCOUTEZ L'ENREGISTREMENT, PUIS COCHEZ LES BONNES RÉPONSES.

Maya ✓ Ben ☐

① Maya ☐ Ben ☐

② Maya ☐ Ben ☐

③ Maya ☐ Ben ☐

④ Maya ☐ Ben ☐

 28.5 LISEZ LES ANNONCES, PUIS COCHEZ LES BONNES RÉPONSES.

Riverside Apartment has four bedrooms.
True ☐ **False** ✓

① Riverside Apartment has one bathroom.
True ☐ **False** ☐

② Lake View has a yard.
True ☐ **False** ☐

③ Lake View has a garage.
True ☐ **False** ☐

④ Stone Hill has five bedrooms.
True ☐ **False** ☐

⑤ Stone Hill has a shower.
True ☐ **False** ☐

⑥ Stone Hill has a kitchen.
True ☐ **False** ☐

34 ACCOMMODATION

PROPERTIES TO RENT

Riverside Apartment $800/month
This old apartment is on the first floor of Riverside House. It has three bedrooms and two bathrooms. There's a beautiful park next door.

Lake View $900/month
This house is on a quiet street next to a lake. It has two bedrooms and a big kitchen in the basement. It also has a beautiful yard, but there is no garage.

Stone Hill $1,500/month
This house is in the old part of Bridgewater. It has four bedrooms and a bathroom with a bathtub and a shower. It also has a big kitchen. All the furniture is new and stylish.

28.6 POINT CLÉ « HAVE » ET LA FORME NÉGATIVE

Bien que « to have » soit un verbe irrégulier, sa forme négative se construit
de manière habituelle. Comme les autres verbes, cette forme négative
a également une forme contractée.

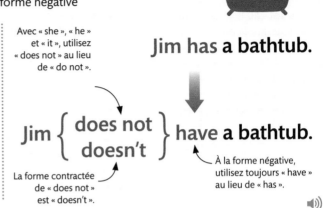

I have a bathtub.

Avec « she », « he »
et « it », utilisez
« does not » au lieu
de « do not ».

Jim has a bathtub.

$$I \begin{Bmatrix} \textbf{do not} \\ \textbf{don't} \end{Bmatrix} \textbf{have a bathtub.}$$

La forme contractée
de « do not » est « don't ».

$$Jim \begin{Bmatrix} \textbf{does not} \\ \textbf{doesn't} \end{Bmatrix} \textbf{have a bathtub.}$$

La forme contractée
de « does not »
est « doesn't ».

À la forme négative,
utilisez toujours « have »
au lieu de « has ».

28.7 RÉCRIVEZ CHAQUE PHRASE AVEC UNE AUTRE FORME NÉGATIVE.

I do not have a car.
I don't have a car.

❶ Kaleh doesn't have a dog.

_____

❷ You do not have a microwave.

_____

❸ Greendale doesn't have a church.

_____

❹ Alyssa and Logan do not have a garage.

_____

❺ We don't have a yard.

_____

28.8 UTILISEZ LE SCHÉMA POUR CRÉER 11 PHRASES, PUIS LISEZ-LES À VOIX HAUTE.

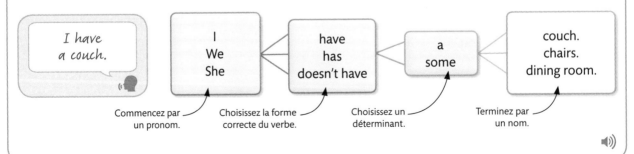

I have a couch.

| I / We / She | have / has / doesn't have | a / some | couch. / chairs. / dining room. |

Commencez par un pronom.

Choisissez la forme correcte du verbe.

Choisissez un déterminant.

Terminez par un nom.

28.9 DIRE AUTREMENT « HAVE »

Certains anglophones (surtout au Royaume-Uni) utilisent « have got » au lieu de « have ». Cela veut dire la même chose.

We { have / have got } a dog.

La seule différence est le mot « got ».

◀))

28.10 CONSTRUCTION « HAVE GOT »

FORME AFFIRMATIVE	FORME NÉGATIVE
I have got a dog.	**He has not got a dog.**
⬇	⬇
I've got a dog.	**He hasn't got a dog.**

On utilise seulement cette forme lorsque « have » est accompagné de « got ». On ne peut pas changer « I have a dog » en « I've a dog ».

La forme contractée « hasn't got » peut être utilisée pour « has not got ».

◀))

 28.11 RÉCRIVEZ CHAQUE PHRASE DE 2 MANIÈRES DIFFÉRENTES.

She has a computer.	She has got a computer.	She's got a computer.
① They don't have a couch.		
② He has three sisters.		
③ You don't have a bike.		
④ We have a microwave.		
⑤ It has a bathtub.		
⑥ They have a cat.		

28 ✓ CHECK-LIST

 « Have » ☐   **Aa** Les objets dans la maison ☐   Parler de ce que vous possèdez ☐

105

Posez des questions avec « have » pour demander à quelqu'un ce qu'il possède. On utilise « do » ou « does » pour formuler la question.

 **Grammaire** Les questions avec « have »

Aa Vocabulaire La maison et le mobilier

Compétence Poser des questions concernant les objets de la maison

---

29.1 POINT CLÉ LES QUESTIONS AVEC « HAVE »

Formulez des questions avec « have » en ajoutant « do » ou « does ».

Quand on pose une question, « has » se transforme en « have ».

You have **a TV.**

She has **a TV.**

Do you have **a TV?**

Does she have **a TV?**

Ajoutez « do » pour transformer les affirmations avec « I », « you », « we » et « they » en questions.

Ajoutez « does » pour transformer les affirmations avec « he », « she » et « it » en questions.

29.2 VOCABULAIRE LES OBJETS DE LA MAISON

toaster

microwave

washing machine

dishwasher

kettle

plate

bowl

cup

silverware (US)
cutlery (UK)

knife

fork

spoon

29.3 TRANSFORMEZ LES AFFIRMATIONS EN QUESTIONS.

> She has an oven.
> _Does she have an oven?_

1 They have a toaster.

_____

2 You have a new couch.

_____

3 Ben has a washing machine.

_____

4 We have an old armchair.

_____

5 Karen has a large TV.

_____

6 The kitchen has a sink.

_____

7 The house has a yard.

_____

🔊

29.4 ÉCOUTEZ, PUIS COCHEZ LE NOM DE LA PERSONNE À QUI L'OBJET APPARTIENT.

Tim ✓   Lucy ☐

3   Tim ☐   Lucy ☐

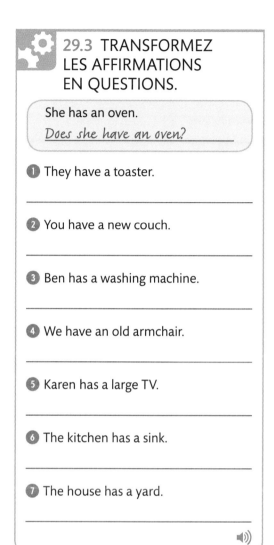

1   Tim ☐   Lucy ☐

4   Tim ☐   Lucy ☐

2   Tim ☐   Lucy ☐

5   Tim ☐   Lucy ☐

29.5 UTILISEZ LE SCHÉMA POUR CRÉER 9 PHRASES, PUIS LISEZ-LES À VOIX HAUTE.

> _Do you have any chairs?_ 🗣

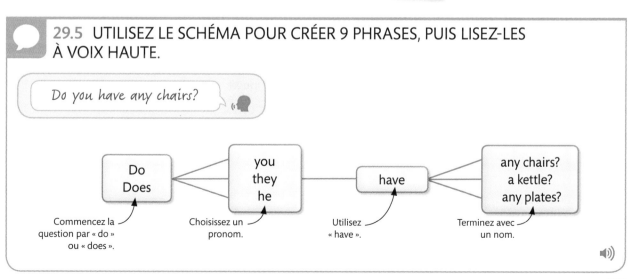

| Do / Does | you / they / he | have | any chairs? / a kettle? / any plates? |

Commencez la question par « do » ou « does ». — Choisissez un pronom. — Utilisez « have ». — Terminez avec un nom.

🔊

107

29.6 POINT CLÉ LES RÉPONSES COURTES AUX QUESTIONS AVEC « HAVE »

Pour répondre aux questions avec « have », vous pouvez utiliser des réponses courtes avec « do » ou « don't ».

Ajoutez « do » pour formuler une question.

Do you have a microwave?

Utilisez « do » dans les réponses affirmatives.

Yes, I do.

No, I don't.

Utilisez « do not » ou « don't » dans les réponses négatives.

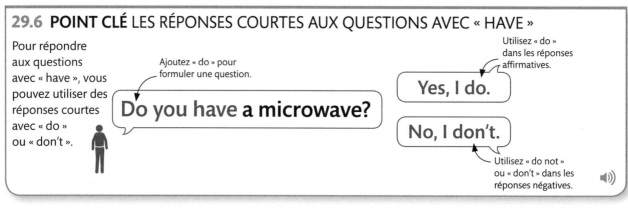

29.7 ÉTUDIEZ L'IMAGE, PUIS RÉPONDEZ AUX QUESTIONS AVEC DES RÉPONSES COURTES.

Do you have a kettle?

Yes, I do.

❶ Do you have a fork?

_____

❷ Do you have a spoon?

_____

❸ Do you have a toaster?

_____

❹ Do you have a microwave?

_____

29.8 ÉTUDIEZ L'IMAGE, PUIS RÉPONDEZ AUX QUESTIONS À VOIX HAUTE.

Does Noah have a dog?

Yes, he does.

❶ Does he have a TV?

❷ Does he have a bookcase?

❸ Does he have a couch?

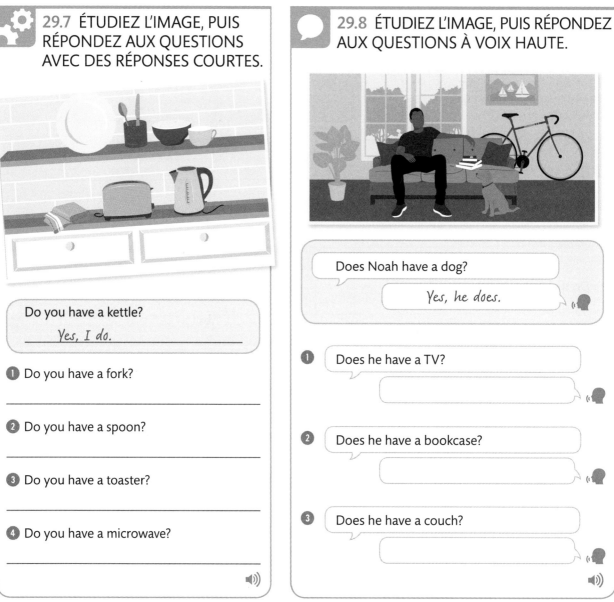

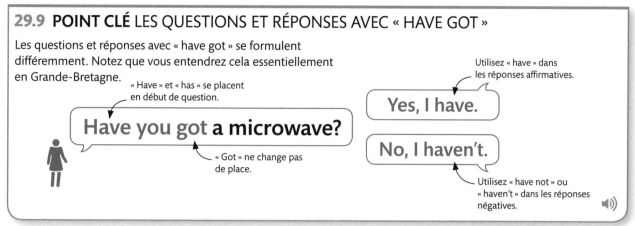

29.9 POINT CLÉ LES QUESTIONS ET RÉPONSES AVEC « HAVE GOT »

Les questions et réponses avec « have got » se formulent différemment. Notez que vous entendrez cela essentiellement en Grande-Bretagne.

« Have » et « has » se placent en début de question.

Have you got a microwave?

« Got » ne change pas de place.

Utilisez « have » dans les réponses affirmatives.

Yes, I have.

No, I haven't.

Utilisez « have not » ou « haven't » dans les réponses négatives.

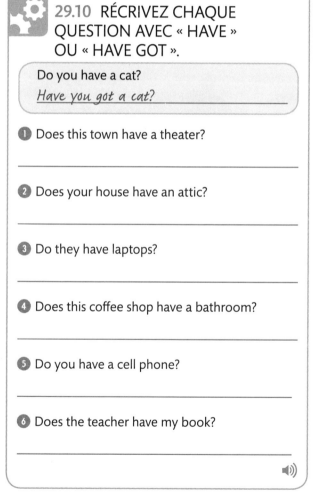

29.10 RÉCRIVEZ CHAQUE QUESTION AVEC « HAVE » OU « HAVE GOT ».

Do you have a cat?
Have you got a cat?

1 Does this town have a theater?
_____

2 Does your house have an attic?
_____

3 Do they have laptops?
_____

4 Does this coffee shop have a bathroom?
_____

5 Do you have a cell phone?
_____

6 Does the teacher have my book?
_____

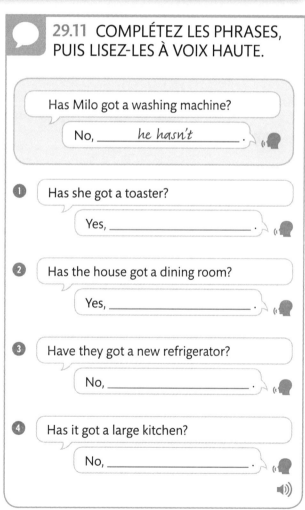

29.11 COMPLÉTEZ LES PHRASES, PUIS LISEZ-LES À VOIX HAUTE.

Has Milo got a washing machine?
No, _____ he hasn't _____.

1 Has she got a toaster?
Yes, _____.

2 Has the house got a dining room?
Yes, _____.

3 Have they got a new refrigerator?
No, _____.

4 Has it got a large kitchen?
No, _____.

30 Vocabulaire

30.1 BOIRE ET MANGER

food

drinks

breakfast

lunch

dinner

meat

fish

seafood

fruit

vegetables

bread

pasta

rice

noodles

potatoes

milk

cheese

butter

yogurt

eggs

sugar

cookie (US)
biscuit (UK)

chocolate

cake

cereal

orange

apple

banana

strawberry

mango

sandwich

burger

fries (US)
chips (UK)

spaghetti

salad

coffee

tea

juice

water

lemonade

31 Compter

En anglais, les noms peuvent être soit dénombrables, soit indénombrables. Les noms dénombrables peuvent être comptés individuellement. Les noms qui ne peuvent pas être séparés et comptés sont indénombrables.

⚙ **Grammaire** Les noms indénombrables
Aa Vocabulaire Les récipients alimentaires
🧩 **Compétence** Parler de nourriture

31.1 POINT CLÉ LES NOMS DÉNOMBRABLES ET INDÉNOMBRABLES

Utilisez « a », « an » ou un nombre pour parler de noms dénombrables. On peut utiliser « some » à la fois pour des noms dénombrables et indénombrables.

NOMS DÉNOMBRABLES	NOMS INDÉNOMBRABLES

There is an egg.

There are four eggs.

There are some eggs.

Utilisez « some » lorsqu'il y a plus de choses dénombrables que vous ne pouvez en compter.

Les noms indénombrables sont toujours accompagnés de verbes au singulier.

There is some rice.

Utilisez toujours « some » avec les noms indénombrables, et non pas « a », « an » ou un nombre.

31.2 AUTRES EXEMPLES LES NOMS DÉNOMBRABLES ET INDÉNOMBRABLES

 a **sandwich**   an **apple**   some **milk**   some **water**

 four **bananas**   two **burgers**   some **spaghetti**   some **sugar**

31.3 BARREZ LE MOT INCORRECT DANS CHAQUE PHRASE.

 Michael has ~~two~~ / some milk.

① Jake has an / some apple.

② There is a / some coffee.

③ Reena eats a / some spaghetti.

④ There are two / some eggs.

⑤ I've got a / some bananas.

31.4 POINT CLÉ LES QUESTIONS ET LA FORME NÉGATIVE

Utilisez « any » dans les phrases négatives et dans les questions pour les noms à la fois dénombrables et indénombrables.

NOMS DÉNOMBRABLES	NOMS INDÉNOMBRABLES

There are some eggs.
Utilisez « are » dans les phrases affirmatives dénombrables.

There aren't any eggs.
Utilisez « aren't » dans les phrases négatives dénombrables.

Are there any eggs?
Utilisez « are there » dans les phrases interrogatives dénombrables.

There is some rice.
Utilisez « is » dans les phrases affirmatives indénombrables.

There isn't any rice.
Utilisez « isn't » dans les phrases négatives indénombrables.

Is there any rice?
Utilisez « is there » dans les phrases interrogatives indénombrables.

31.5 COMPLÉTEZ AVEC LES FORMES AFFIRMATIVES, NÉGATIVES OU INTERROGATIVES MANQUANTES.

Are there any bananas?	There are some bananas.	There aren't any bananas.
❶ Is there any milk?		
❷	There is some chocolate.	
❸		There aren't any apples.

31.6 RÉPONDEZ AUX QUESTIONS, PUIS LISEZ LES RÉPONSES À VOIX HAUTE.

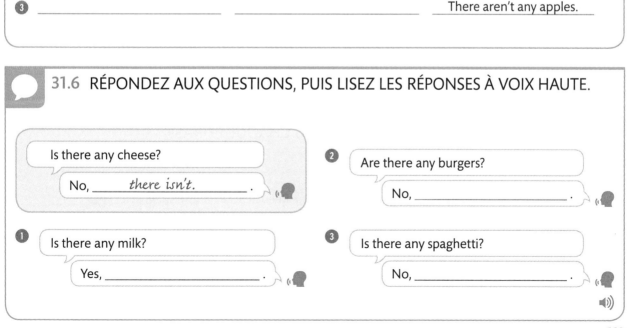

Is there any cheese?
No, _____ *there isn't.* _____ .

❷ Are there any burgers?
No, _____ .

❶ Is there any milk?
Yes, _____ .

❸ Is there any spaghetti?
No, _____ .

31.7 VOCABULAIRE LES RÉCIPIENTS ALIMENTAIRES

box

bottle

bag

bar

tube

glass

carton

jar

31.8 POINT CLÉ TRANSFORMER LES INDÉNOMBRABLES EN DÉNOMBRABLES

Ce qui est indénombrable peut devenir dénombrable s'il est placé dans un récipient.

some sugar ➡ a bag of sugar

some water ➡ three bottles of water

some cereal ➡ a bowl of cereal

31.9 OBSERVEZ LES IMAGES, PUIS COMPLÉTEZ LES PHRASES.

There is ___a jar of___ coffee.

1 There is _____ flour.

2 There is _____ coffee.

3 There is _____ juice.

4 There are _____ spaghetti.

5 There are _____ milk.

31.10 POINT CLÉ LES QUESTIONS CONCERNANT LES QUANTITÉS

On utilise « many » pour poser des questions concernant les quantités de noms dénombrables
et « much » pour poser des questions concernant les quantités de noms indénombrables.

How many eggs are there?

Utilisez « many » avec un nom
au pluriel dans les questions
dénombrables.

How much rice is there?

Utilisez « much » avec un nom
au singulier dans les questions
indénombrables.

31.11 AUTRES EXEMPLES LES NOMS DÉNOMBRABLES ET INDÉNOMBRABLES

How many cupcakes are there?

How many apples are there?

How much pasta is there?

How much chocolate is there?

31.12 COMPLÉTEZ LES PHRASES AVEC « HOW MUCH » OU « HOW MANY ».

How much pizza is there?

❶ _____ glasses of juice are there?

❷ _____ water is there?

❸ _____ potatoes are there?

❹ _____ bars of chocolate are there?

❺ _____ pasta is there?

❻ _____ cartons of juice are there?

❼ _____ milk is there?

31.13 ÉCOUTEZ L'ENREGISTREMENT ET COCHEZ LES BONNES RÉPONSES.

Écoutez Mila et Jon qui préparent
leur liste de courses.

How many pizzas are there?
one ☐ two ☑ three ☐

❶ How much flour do they need?
two bags ☐ one bag ☐ three bags ☐

❷ How many cartons of juice are there?
one ☐ three ☐ five ☐

❸ How much coffee is there?
none ☐ some ☐

❹ They need some...
sausages ☐ cheese ☐ burgers. ☐

31 ✓ CHECK-LIST

⚙ Les noms indénombrables ☐   **Aa** Les récipients alimentaires ☐   🧩 Parler de nourriture ☐

32 Mesurer

Utilisez « enough » lorsque vous avez un nombre exact ou une quantité exacte. Utilisez « too many » ou « too much » pour dire « trop ».

⚙ **Grammaire** Les mesures
Aa Vocabulaire Les ingrédients et les quantités
🧩 **Compétence** Parler de quantités

32.1 POINT CLÉ « ENOUGH » ET « TOO MANY »

Utilisez « enough », « not enough » et « too many » pour parler des quantités des noms dénombrables.

Les œufs sont dénombrables.

We need four eggs. Do we have enough?

Utilisez « enough » dans les questions.

We have two eggs. That's not enough.
Vous avez besoin de 4 œufs ; 2 ne suffisent pas.

We have four eggs. That's enough.
La quantité correcte est 4 œufs : cela suffit.

We have five eggs. That's too many.
5 œufs sont plus qu'assez : il y en a trop.

🔊

32.2 AUTRES EXEMPLES « ENOUGH » ET « TOO MANY »

There are enough eggs.

You have enough eggs.

There aren't enough eggs.

You don't have enough eggs.

There are too many eggs.

You have too many eggs.

🔊

32.3 LISEZ LA RECETTE DE CUISINE, PUIS BARREZ LES MOTS INCORRECTS.

There ~~aren't enough~~ / are too many mangoes.

FRUIT SALAD RECIPE
2 apples
4 oranges
1 pineapple
3 bananas
1 mango

❶ There aren't enough / are enough oranges.

❷ You have enough / too many pineapples.

❸ There aren't enough / are too many apples.

❹ You don't have enough / too many bananas.

🔊

32.4 POINT CLÉ « ENOUGH » ET « TOO MUCH »

Utilisez « enough »,
« not enough »
et « too much »
pour parler des
quantités des noms
indénombrables.

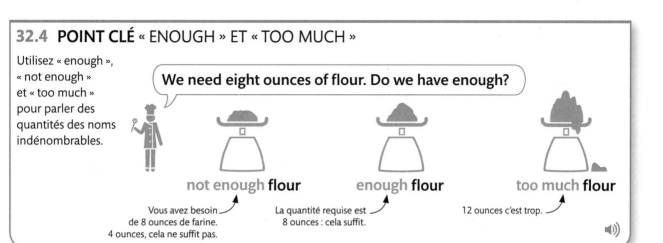

We need eight ounces of flour. Do we have enough?

not enough **flour**

enough **flour**

too much **flour**

Vous avez besoin
de 8 ounces de farine.
4 ounces, cela ne suffit pas.

La quantité requise est
8 ounces : cela suffit.

12 ounces c'est trop.

32.5 AUTRES EXEMPLES « ENOUGH » ET « TOO MUCH »

There is enough flour.

There isn't enough flour.

There is too much flour.

They have enough flour.

They don't have enough flour.

They have too much flour.

32.6 ÉCOUTEZ L'ENREGISTREMENT, PUIS RELIEZ CHAQUE IMAGE À LA QUANTITÉ CORRESPONDANTE.

Sheila et Vikram préparent les
ingrédients pour faire un gâteau.

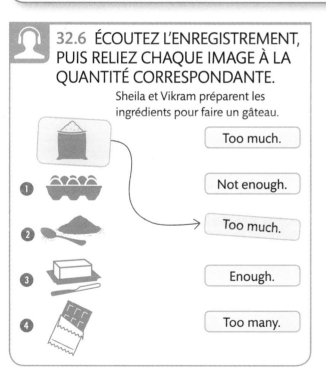

Too much.

Not enough.

Too much.

Enough.

Too many.

32.7 BARREZ LE MOT INCORRECT DANS CHAQUE PHRASE.

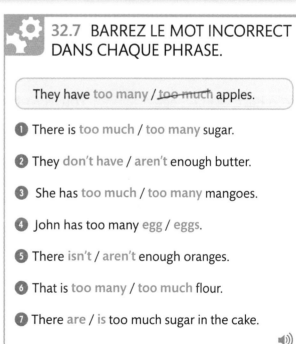

They have too many / ~~too much~~ apples.

1 There is too much / too many sugar.

2 They don't have / aren't enough butter.

3 She has too much / too many mangoes.

4 John has too many egg / eggs.

5 There isn't / aren't enough oranges.

6 That is too many / too much flour.

7 There are / is too much sugar in the cake.

---

32 ✓ CHECK-LIST

⚙️ Les mesures ☐   **Aa** Les ingrédients et les quantités ☐   🧩 Parler de quantités ☐

33.1 LES VÊTEMENTS ET LES ACCESSOIRES

t-shirt

blouse

shirt

dress

skirt

pants (US)
trousers (UK)

jeans

jacket

coat

raincoat

socks

boots

shoes

sandals

sneakers (US)
trainers (UK)

scarf

hat

gloves

belt

purse (US)
handbag (UK)

33.2 LES TAILLES VESTIMENTAIRES

extra small	small	medium	large	extra large
....	....	....	....	....

33.3 DÉCRIRE LES VÊTEMENTS

 short sleeves   long sleeves

....

 cheap   expensive

smart	casual	suit	uniform	cheap	expensive
....	....	....	....	....	....

33.4 LES COULEURS

red	orange	yellow	green	blue
....	....	....	....	....

purple	pink	white	gray (US) grey (UK)	black
....	....	....	....	....

34 Dans les magasins

Plusieurs verbes sont à votre disposition pour parler de ce qui se passe lorsque vous faites des achats. Utilisez « too » et « enough » pour dire comment des vêtements vous vont.

⚙ **Grammaire** « Too » et « fit »
Aa Vocabulaire Les magasins et les vêtements
🧩 **Compétence** Décrire des vêtements

34.1 VOCABULAIRE LES VERBES DU SHOPPING

Ana owns a red hat.

....

Choose a new shirt!

....

Luc sells old clothes.

....

They want new shoes.

....

The hat fits Jane.

....

Let's buy some hats!

....

 ## 34.2 BARREZ LE MOT INCORRECT DANS CHAQUE PHRASE.

Tsuru ~~want~~ / **wants** a green jumper.

1 Hannah **choose** / **chooses** a yellow skirt.

2 Elliot and Ruby **buy** / **buys** a new couch.

3 Sue **own** / **owns** an old winter coat.

4 Jess's dad **buy** / **buys** her a new bike.

5 Chris and Lisa **own** / **owns** a black sports car.

6 Gayle and Mike **sell** / **sells** shoes at the market.

7 Mia **choose** / **chooses** her red shoes.

8 The shoes **fit** / **fits** me.

9 We **want** / **wants** new white shirts.

34.3 ÉCRIVEZ LES MOTS SUIVANTS DANS LE BON ORDRE AFIN DE RECONSTITUER LES PHRASES.

She | a | green | long | dress | buys

She buys a long green dress.

① They | expensive | sweaters. | blue | choose

_____

② some | brown | old | hats. | has | Judith

_____

③ sells | This | shop | short | red | pants.

_____

④ owns | Tina | black | cheap | shoes.

_____

⑤ Jim | buys | black | new | a | coat

_____

Aa 34.4 LISEZ LES MESSAGES, PUIS ENTOUREZ 12 ADJECTIFS.

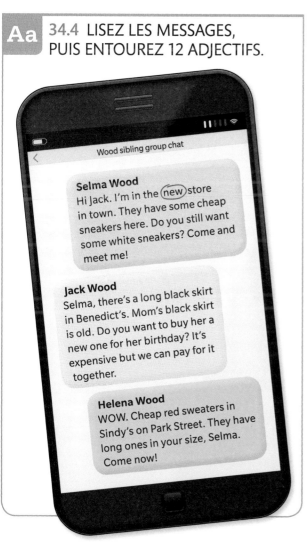

Wood sibling group chat

Selma Wood
Hi Jack. I'm in the (new) store in town. They have some cheap sneakers here. Do you still want some white sneakers? Come and meet me!

Jack Wood
Selma, there's a long black skirt in Benedict's. Mom's black skirt is old. Do you want to buy her a new one for her birthday? It's expensive but we can pay for it together.

Helena Wood
WOW. Cheap red sweaters in Sindy's on Park Street. They have long ones in your size, Selma. Come now!

34.5 ÉCOUTEZ, PUIS COCHEZ LES BONNES RÉPONSES.

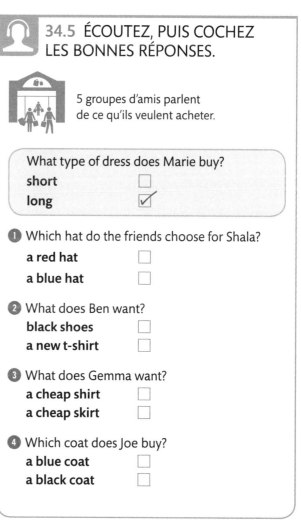

5 groupes d'amis parlent de ce qu'ils veulent acheter.

What type of dress does Marie buy?
short ☐
long ☑

① Which hat do the friends choose for Shala?
a red hat ☐
a blue hat ☐

② What does Ben want?
black shoes ☐
a new t-shirt ☐

③ What does Gemma want?
a cheap shirt ☐
a cheap skirt ☐

④ Which coat does Joe buy?
a blue coat ☐
a black coat ☐

34.6 POINT CLÉ RÉPONDRE À LA QUESTION « DOES IT FIT ? »

En anglais, on utilise « enough » et « too » suivi d'un adjectif
pour dire comment un vêtement vous va.

Le nom vient en premier lorsqu'on demande
si un vêtement est à la bonne taille.

Does the sweater fit?

No, it is not big enough.

Is the sweater too small?

No, it is big enough.

Does the sweater fit?

No, it is too big.

Aa 34.7 RELIEZ LES EXPRESSIONS QUI ONT LE MÊME SENS.

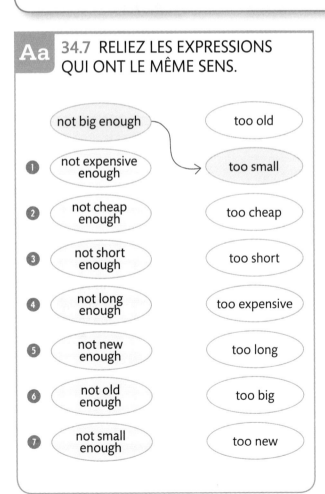

not big enough → too small

too old

1. not expensive enough
2. not cheap enough → too cheap
3. not short enough → too short
4. not long enough → too expensive
5. not new enough → too long
6. not old enough → too big
7. not small enough → too new

34.8 COMPLÉTEZ LES PHRASES AVEC LES MOTS DE LA LISTE.

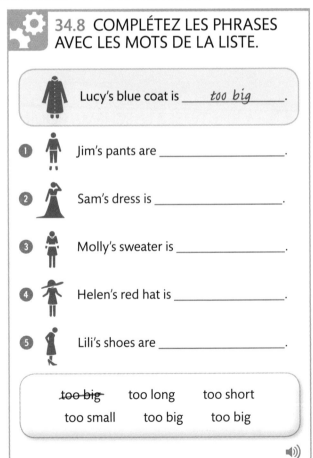

Lucy's blue coat is ___*too big*___.

1. Jim's pants are _____.
2. Sam's dress is _____.
3. Molly's sweater is _____.
4. Helen's red hat is _____.
5. Lili's shoes are _____.

~~too big~~   too long   too short
too small   too big   too big

34.9 ÉCOUTEZ L'ENREGISTREMENT, PUIS COCHEZ CE QUE CHAQUE PERSONNE DÉCRIT.

34.10 UTILISEZ LE SCHÉMA POUR CRÉER 12 PHRASES, PUIS LISEZ-LES À VOIX HAUTE.

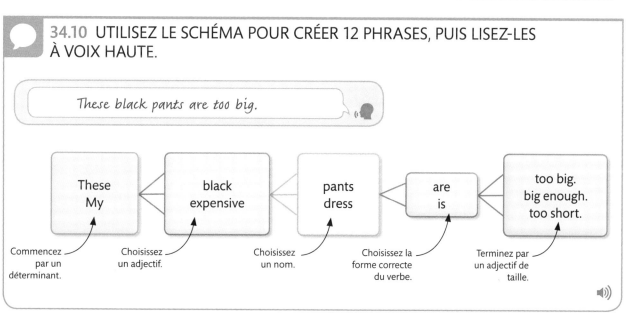

These black pants are *too big.*

These / My	black / expensive	pants / dress	are / is	too big. / big enough. / too short.
Commencez par un déterminant.	Choisissez un adjectif.	Choisissez un nom.	Choisissez la forme correcte du verbe.	Terminez par un adjectif de taille.

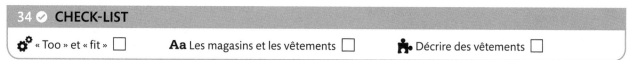

34 ✅ CHECK-LIST

⚙️ « Too » et « fit » ☐   **Aa** Les magasins et les vêtements ☐   🧩 Décrire des vêtements ☐

35 Décrire des choses

Vous pouvez utiliser des adjectifs pour exprimer
votre opinion ou donner des précisions.
On peut mettre plusieurs adjectifs devant un nom.

⚙ **Grammaire** Les adjectifs de l'opinion
Aa Vocabulaire Les magasins et les matériaux
🧩 **Compétence** Donner votre opinion

35.1 POINT CLÉ LES ADJECTIFS EXPRIMANT L'OPINION

Certains adjectifs permettent de donner une opinion plutôt que de présenter des faits.

This is a { great / lovely / fun / beautiful } **hat.**

Ces adjectifs sont positifs.

It is a / an { horrible / terrible / boring / ugly } **hat.**

Ces adjectifs sont négatifs.

35.2 POINT CLÉ L'ORDRE DES ADJECTIFS

En anglais, les adjectifs suivent généralement un ordre précis.
Les adjectifs de l'opinion se placent avant les adjectifs factuels.

	ADJECTIF DE L'OPINION	ADJECTIF FACTUEL	NOM
This is a	**lovely**	**green**	**hat.**

Les adjectifs de l'opinion se placent en premier.

Les adjectifs factuels se placent en dernier.

35.3 AUTRES EXEMPLES L'ORDRE DES ADJECTIFS

 It is a lovely big house.

 Natalie has a beautiful old cat.

 We have a horrible old car.

 They are ugly purple shoes.

 This is a great new book.

 He is a brilliant young actor.

Aa 35.4 BARREZ L'ADJECTIF INCORRECT DANS CHAQUE PHRASE.

It is a good / ~~bad~~ young dog.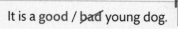

1 This is a **lovely** / **horrible** old t-shirt.

2 This is a **boring** / **great** movie.

3 I have a **lovely** / **horrible** long dress.

4 This is a **beautiful** / **ugly** bird.

5 This is a **fun** / **boring** party.

35.5 ÉCRIVEZ LES MOTS DANS LE BON ORDRE AFIN DE RECONSTITUER LES PHRASES.

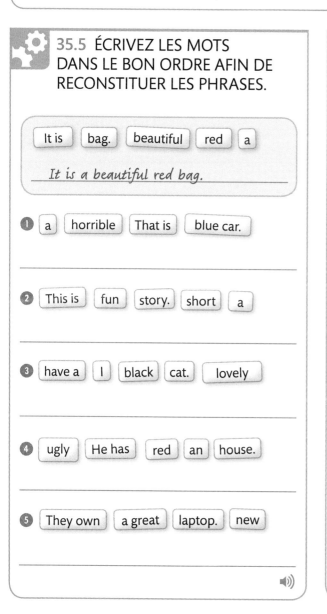

It is   bag.   beautiful   red   a

It is a beautiful red bag.

1 a   horrible   That is   blue car.

_____

2 This is   fun   story.   short   a

_____

3 have a   I   black   cat.   lovely

_____

4 ugly   He has   red   an   house.

_____

5 They own   a great   laptop.   new

_____

35.6 ÉCOUTEZ L'ENREGISTREMENT, PUIS COCHEZ LA BONNE RÉPONSE.

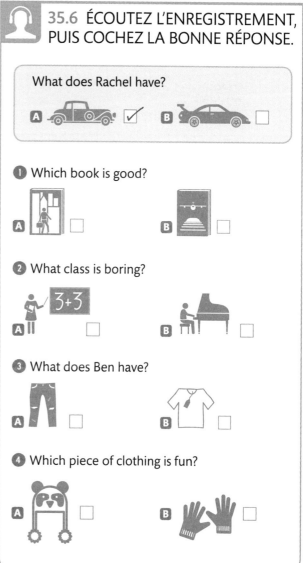

What does Rachel have?

A ☑   B ☐

1 Which book is good?

A ☐   B ☐

2 What class is boring?

A ☐   B ☐

3 What does Ben have?

A ☐   B ☐

4 Which piece of clothing is fun?

A ☐   B ☐

35.7 VOCABULAIRE LES MATÉRIAUX

Certains mots peuvent être utilisés comme noms pour décrire un matériau ou comme adjectifs pour indiquer de quoi les objets sont faits. Deux noms changent lorsqu'ils deviennent adjectifs : le nom « wood » devient l'adjectif « wooden » et le nom « wool » devient l'adjectif « woolen ».

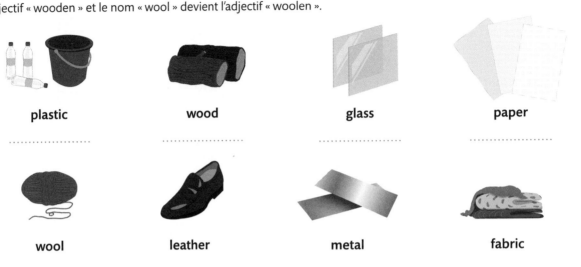

plastic

wood

glass

paper

wool

leather

metal

fabric

Aa 35.8 RELIEZ CHAQUE IMAGE À LA DESCRIPTION CORRESPONDANTE.

Oh, no, the blue glass vase!

That's an expensive leather couch.

This is a beautiful wooden table.

What an interesting metal box!

We have two plastic chairs.

35.9 RECTIFIEZ L'ORDRE DES MOTS, ÉCRIVEZ LES PHRASES, PUIS LISEZ-LES À VOIX HAUTE.

We have lovely two purple couches.

We have two lovely purple couches.

❶ She owns some wooden beautiful chairs.

❷ We own don't those plastic plates horrible.

❸ They have yellow an ugly car.

❹ He wears a blue boring sweater.

❺ She wants a metal lamp new.

❻ He owns a fabric large bag.

❼ Norah new a leather wants jacket.

---

35 ✓ CHECK-LIST

⚙ Les adjectifs de l'opinion ☐   **Aa** Les magasins et les matériaux ☐   🧩 Donner votre opinion ☐

🔄 BILAN L'ANGLAIS QUE VOUS AVEZ APPRIS DANS LES CHAPITRES 27-35

NOUVEAU POINT LINGUISTIQUE	EXEMPLE TYPE	☑	CHAPITRE
« HAVE »	I have **a garage.** She has **a yard.** I do not **have a bathtub.**	☐	28.1, 28.6
POSER DES QUESTIONS AVEC « HAVE »	Do you have a TV?	☐	29.1
LES NOMS DÉNOMBRABLES ET INDÉNOMBRABLES	There are four **eggs.** There is some **rice.** Are there any **eggs?** Is there any **rice?**	☐	31.1, 31.4
« ENOUGH » ET « MANY »	We have enough **eggs.** We have too many **eggs.**	☐	32.1
LES VERBES DU SHOPPING	Ana owns **a red hat.** Luc sells **old clothes.** They want **new shoes.** The hat fits **Jane.**	☐	34.1
L'ORDRE DES ADJECTIFS	This is a lovely green **hat.**	☐	35.1

36.1 LES SPORTS

swimming

sailing

skateboarding

running

skiing

snowboarding

roller-skating

surfing

tennis

golf

badminton

baseball

basketball

soccer (US)
football (UK)

football (US)
American
football (UK)

rugby

volleyball

cycling

ice hockey

horse riding

36.2 LES ÉQUIPEMENTS

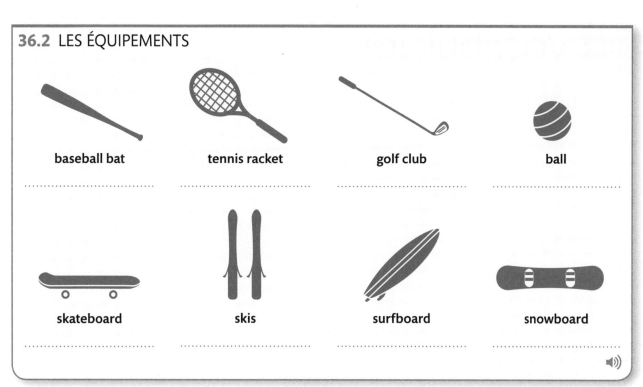

baseball bat

tennis racket

golf club

ball

skateboard

skis

surfboard

snowboard

36.3 LES INSTALLATIONS

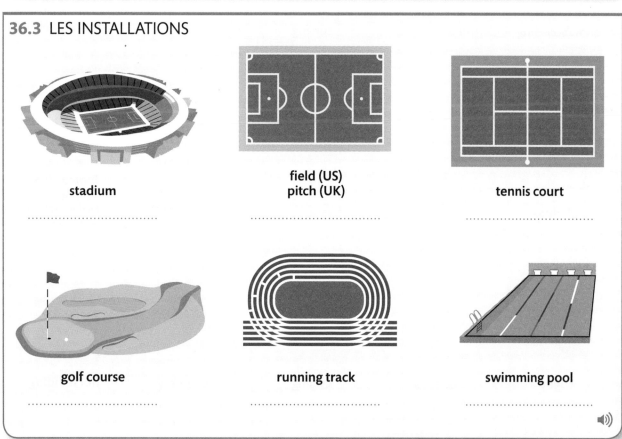

stadium

field (US)
pitch (UK)

tennis court

golf course

running track

swimming pool

37 Parler de sport

Pour parler des sports auxquels vous participez, utilisez le verbe « to go » suivi du gérondif. Pour les autres sports, utilisez « to play » suivi d'un nom.

⚙ **Grammaire** « Go » et « play »
Aa Vocabulaire Les sports
🧩 **Compétence** Parler de sport

37.1 POINT CLÉ « GO » SUIVI DU GÉRONDIF

Vous pouvez ajouter « -ing » au radical du verbe qui suit « go ». On appelle cette forme le gérondif.

« Go » change en fonction du sujet.

She goes surfing on the weekend.

Ajoutez « -ing » au radical du verbe.

🔊

37.2 AUTRES EXEMPLES « GO » SUIVI DU GÉRONDIF

I go swimming **once a week.**

He goes skateboarding **twice a month.**

Do they go dancing **on Saturday nights?**

We don't **go fishing at the lake.**

He doesn't **go cycling with his brothers.**

Does she **go sailing in the summer?**

🔊

⚙ 37.3 COMPLÉTEZ LES PHRASES.

Tamara _____ *goes* _____ swimming in the sea.

 1 We don't _____ surfing in the winter.

 2 Do you _____ sailing on the weekend?

 3 Tipo _____ cycling five times a week.

 4 He _____ fishing on the river.

 5 Sharon _____ dancing with her friend.

 6 Do they _____ running every morning?

7 He doesn't _____ horse riding.

🔊

37.4 ÉCOUTEZ L'ENREGISTREMENT, PUIS RELIEZ LE SPORT AU JOUR CORRESPONDANT.

Monday   Tuesday   Wednesday   Thursday   Friday

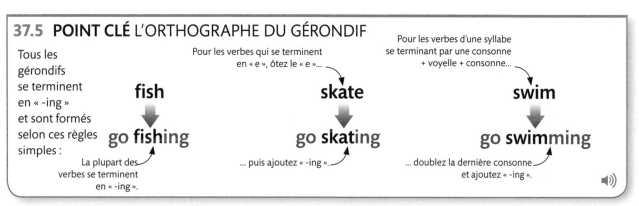

37.5 POINT CLÉ L'ORTHOGRAPHE DU GÉRONDIF

Tous les gérondifs se terminent en « -ing » et sont formés selon ces règles simples :

fish ➤ **go fishing**
La plupart des verbes se terminent en « -ing ».

Pour les verbes qui se terminent en « e », ôtez le « e »...
skate ➤ **go skating**
... puis ajoutez « -ing ».

Pour les verbes d'une syllabe se terminant par une consonne + voyelle + consonne...
swim ➤ **go swimming**
... doublez la dernière consonne et ajoutez « -ing ».

37.6 ENTOUREZ 9 MOTS CACHÉS DANS LA GRILLE, PUIS CLASSEZ-LES.

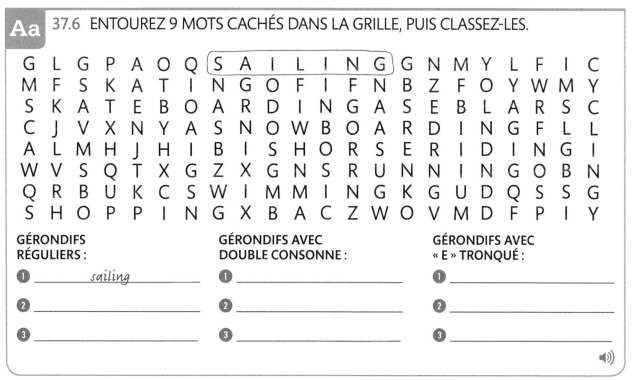

```
G  L  G  P  A  O  Q  S  A  I  L  I  N  G  G  N  M  Y  L  F  I  C
M  F  S  K  A  T  I  N  G  O  F  I  F  N  B  Z  F  O  Y  W  M  Y
S  K  A  T  E  B  O  A  R  D  I  N  G  A  S  E  B  L  A  R  S  C
C  J  V  X  N  Y  A  S  N  O  W  B  O  A  R  D  I  N  G  F  L  L
A  L  M  H  J  H  I  B  I  S  H  O  R  S  E  R  I  D  I  N  G  I
W  V  S  Q  T  X  G  Z  X  G  N  S  R  U  N  N  I  N  G  O  B  N
Q  R  B  U  K  C  S  W  I  M  M  I  N  G  K  G  U  D  Q  S  S  G
S  H  O  P  P  I  N  G  X  B  A  C  Z  W  O  V  M  D  F  P  I  Y
```

GÉRONDIFS RÉGULIERS :

1. _____ *sailing* _____

2. _____

3. _____

GÉRONDIFS AVEC DOUBLE CONSONNE :

1. _____

2. _____

3. _____

GÉRONDIFS AVEC « E » TRONQUÉ :

1. _____

2. _____

3. _____

37.7 POINT CLÉ « PLAY » AVEC UN NOM

Pour certains sports, essentiellement ceux de balle
et de compétition, on utilise « play » suivi du nom.

 « Play » change en fonction
du sujet.

On place le nom
après le verbe.

They play tennis on Sundays.

37.8 AUTRES EXEMPLES « PLAY » AVEC UN NOM

 I don't play tennis in winter.

 Sala plays golf on Tuesday mornings.

 He plays baseball for the town.

 Do Ben and Si play chess together?

 Does Dani play hockey on Mondays?

 We don't play badminton any more.

37.9 BARREZ LE MOT INCORRECT DANS CHAQUE PHRASE.

I ~~plays~~ / play football in the park.

1. Shala **don't** / **doesn't play** tennis.

2. Mina **plays** / **play** golf at the club.

3. We **plays** / **play** squash on Mondays.

4. The dog **plays** / **play** with its ball.

5. Maria **don't** / **doesn't play** tennis.

6. The kids **don't** / **doesn't play** games at school.

7. They **play** / **plays** soccer at the park.

37.10 RÉCRIVEZ LES PHRASES EN CORRIGEANT LES ERREURS.

He **don't play** hockey in the summer.
He doesn't play hockey in the summer.

1. We **plays** tennis every Tuesday night.

_____

2. They **doesn't play** golf during the week.

_____

3. You **doesn't play** volleyball at the beach.

_____

4. Do they **plays** together every Saturday?

_____

YOUR SPORTS

Littleton's Sports Scene

Some local residents tell us about their sports routines

I go to Belgrade Sports. It's a great place to exercise. I play squash on Mondays and Fridays.
JAMES

I love Highfields Sports. I go swimming five days a week, from Monday to Friday. I play golf on Saturdays and I play tennis on Sundays. I really like it there!
SARA

Lots of my friends go to the park and some of them play football there. I go running there. It's great.
CHAS

I like badminton and skating. I can do both at Littleton Sports. I go swimming there on Tuesdays and Fridays because there's a nice pool, and I play football on Wednesdays.
CASSIE

Who plays squash on Mondays and Fridays?
James ☑   Sara ☐   Chas ☐   Cassie ☐

❶ Who plays golf?
James ☐   Sara ☐   Chas ☐   Cassie ☐

❷ Who goes running in the park?
James ☐   Sara ☐   Chas ☐   Cassie ☐

❸ Who goes swimming on Thursdays?
James ☐   Sara ☐   Chas ☐   Cassie ☐

❹ Who plays badminton?
James ☐   Sara ☐   Chas ☐   Cassie ☐

37.12 COMPLÉTEZ LES PHRASES AVEC « GO » OU « PLAY », PUIS LISEZ-LES À VOIX HAUTE.

I _go dancing_ (dance) with my friends on Mondays.

❶ Milo and I _____ (cycle) in the park on Saturdays.

❷ The team _____ (football) from 6pm to 7pm on Wednesdays.

❸ Imelda _____ (horse ride) once a month.

❹ Luther _____ (fish) during his vacation time.

❺ Hannah _____ (tennis) with her cousin on Monday evenings.

---

37 ✓ CHECK-LIST

⚙ « Go » et « play » ☐   Aa Les sports ☐   🧩 Parler de sport ☐

38.1 LES LOISIRS ET LES PASSE-TEMPS

do puzzles

play cards

play chess

play board games

play computer games /
play video games

read

draw

write

paint

take photos

play a musical
instrument

walk / hike

cook

bake

sew

knit

watch television

watch a movie (US)
watch a film (UK)

see a play

play sport /
do exercise

go to the gym

do yoga

listen to music

go camping

go bird watching

go out for a meal

do the gardening

visit a museum /
art gallery

meet friends

go on vacation (US)
go on holiday (UK)

go sightseeing

go shopping

39 Parler de votre temps libre

Les adverbes de fréquence permettent d'indiquer
la fréquence à laquelle vous effectuez une activité.
On place généralement l'adverbe entre le sujet et le verbe.

⚙ **Grammaire** Les adverbes de fréquence
Aa Vocabulaire Les passe-temps
🧩 **Compétence** Parler de votre temps libre

39.1 VOCABULAIRE LES ADVERBES DE FRÉQUENCE

Utilisez les adverbes
de fréquence pour
indiquer la fréquence
à laquelle vous
effectuez une activité.
L'adverbe se place
généralement entre
le sujet et le verbe.

100%

I **always** watch TV at night.

I **usually** eat dinner at 7pm.

I **often** walk to work unless it's raining.

I **sometimes** go shopping on the weekend.

0% I **never** go to the gym. I'm too lazy!

🔊

39.2 POINT CLÉ LES ADVERBES DE FRÉQUENCE

Les expressions
de temps
avec un adverbe
de fréquence
se placent
souvent à la fin
de la phrase.

SUJET	ADVERBE DE FRÉQUENCE	ACTIVITÉ	EXPRESSION TEMPORE
I	always	watch TV	at night.

39.3 ÉCRIVEZ LES MOTS SUIVANTS DANS LE BON ORDRE AFIN DE RECONSTITUER LES PHRASES.

in the | plays | morning. | tennis | He | always

He always plays tennis in the morning.

❷ usually | cycle | work. | Sally and Ken | to

_____

❶ go | never | to the | mall. | We

_____

❸ sister | My | often | works | outside.

_____

🔊

136

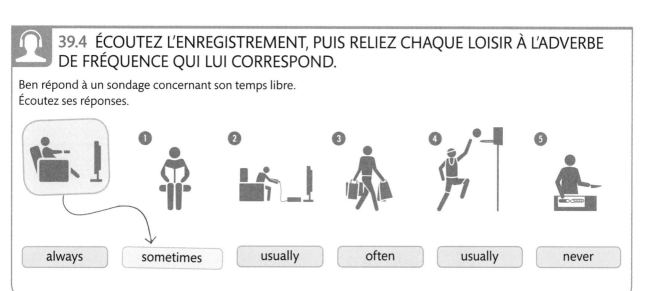

39.4 ÉCOUTEZ L'ENREGISTREMENT, PUIS RELIEZ CHAQUE LOISIR À L'ADVERBE DE FRÉQUENCE QUI LUI CORRESPOND.

Ben répond à un sondage concernant son temps libre.
Écoutez ses réponses.

always sometimes usually often usually never

39.5 COMPLÉTEZ LES PHRASES À L'AIDE DU TABLEAU, PUIS LISEZ-LES À VOIX HAUTE.

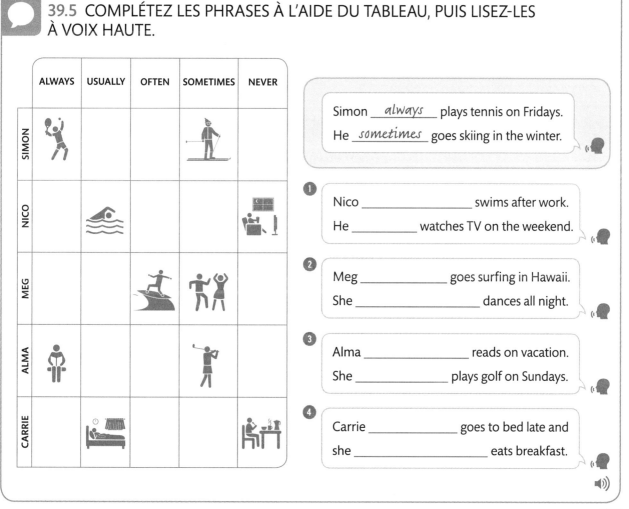

	ALWAYS	USUALLY	OFTEN	SOMETIMES	NEVER
SIMON	🎾			⛷	
NICO		🏊			📺
MEG			🏄	💃	
ALMA	📖			🏌	
CARRIE		🛏			☕

Simon __always__ plays tennis on Fridays.
He __sometimes__ goes skiing in the winter.

① Nico _____ swims after work.
He _____ watches TV on the weekend.

② Meg _____ goes surfing in Hawaii.
She _____ dances all night.

③ Alma _____ reads on vacation.
She _____ plays golf on Sundays.

④ Carrie _____ goes to bed late and
she _____ eats breakfast.

39.6 CONSTRUCTION LES QUESTIONS SUR LE TEMPS LIBRE

Utilisez différents mots interrogatifs pour demander à quelle fréquence
une personne effectue une activité et le moment précis auquel il la réalise.

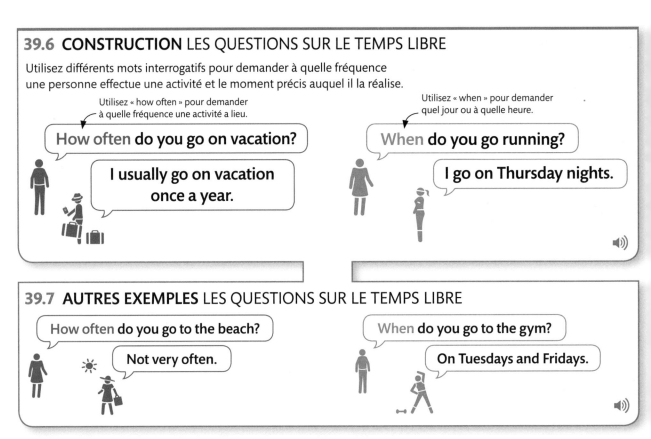

Utilisez « how often » pour demander
à quelle fréquence une activité a lieu.

How often do you go on vacation?

**I usually go on vacation
once a year.**

Utilisez « when » pour demander
quel jour ou à quelle heure.

When do you go running?

I go on Thursday nights.

39.7 AUTRES EXEMPLES LES QUESTIONS SUR LE TEMPS LIBRE

How often do you go to the beach?

Not very often.

When do you go to the gym?

On Tuesdays and Fridays.

39.8 COCHEZ LA RÉPONSE CORRESPONDANT À CHAQUE QUESTION.

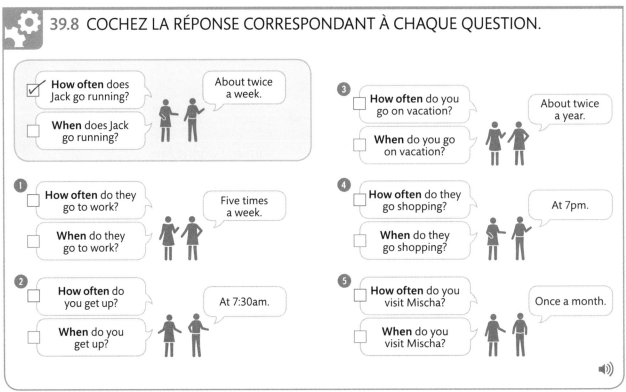

✓ **How often** does
Jack go running?

☐ **When** does Jack
go running?

About twice
a week.

❶ ☐ **How often** do they
go to work?

☐ **When** do they
go to work?

Five times
a week.

❷ ☐ **How often** do
you get up?

☐ **When** do you
get up?

At 7:30am.

❸ ☐ **How often** do you
go on vacation?

☐ **When** do you go
on vacation?

About twice
a year.

❹ ☐ **How often** do they
go shopping?

☐ **When** do they
go shopping?

At 7pm.

❺ ☐ **How often** do you
visit Mischa?

☐ **When** do you
visit Mischa?

Once a month.

39.9 POSEZ LA QUESTION CORRESPONDANT À CHAQUE AFFIRMATION.

She goes dancing twice a week.
How often does she go dancing?

① They visit their grandparents on Saturdays.

_____

② We go skating during the winter.

_____

③ He usually plays hockey three times a month.

_____

④ You go shopping on Fridays.

_____

⑤ They see their parents every weekend.

_____

⑥ He never walks the dog.

_____

⑦ We sometimes go skating on the lake.

_____

🔊

39.10 POSEZ LA QUESTION CORRESPONDANT À CHAQUE AFFIRMATION, PUIS LISEZ-LA À VOIX HAUTE.

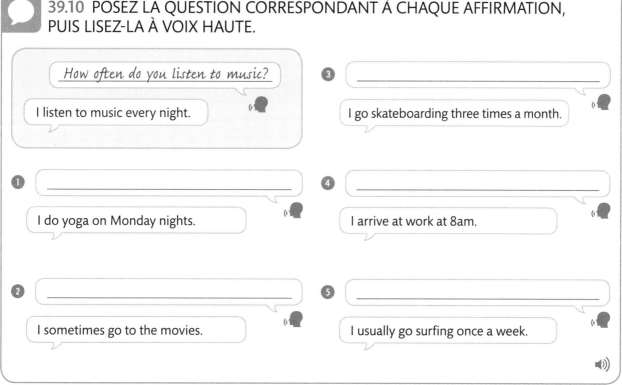

How often do you listen to music?

I listen to music every night.

① _____

I do yoga on Monday nights.

② _____

I sometimes go to the movies.

③ _____

I go skateboarding three times a month.

④ _____

I arrive at work at 8am.

⑤ _____

I usually go surfing once a week.

🔊

39 ✓ CHECK-LIST

⚙ Les adverbes de fréquence ☐   **Aa** Les passe-temps ☐   🧩 Parler de votre temps libre ☐

40 Exprimer vos goûts

Les verbes « to love », « to like » et « to hate » vous permettent d'exprimer ce que vous ressentez. Vous pouvez les utiliser avec un nom ou un gérondif.

⚙ **Grammaire** « Love », « like » et « hate »
Aa **Vocabulaire** La nourriture, les sports et les passe-temps
🧩 **Compétence** Parler de ce que vous aimez

40.1 POINT CLÉ AIMER OU NE PAS AIMER AVEC UN NOM

Vous pouvez utiliser les verbes du goût avec des noms.

Utilisez « do not » ou « don't » et « does not » ou « doesn't » pour exprimer une opinion négative.

CONSEIL
« Don't like » a le même sens que « dislike », mais on utilise davantage « don't like » à l'oral.

She likes tennis.

Max doesn't like pizza.

I love chocolate.

Cela veut dire que vous aimez vraiment le chocolat.

They hate coffee.

Ce verbe est plus fort que « don't like ».

🔊

40.2 AUTRES EXEMPLES AIMER OU NE PAS AIMER AVEC UN NOM

I love fries.

You don't like baseball.

The cat doesn't like its food.

Oliver hates board games.

🔊

⚙ 40.3 RELIEZ CHAQUE IMAGE À LA DESCRIPTION CORRESPONDANTE.

Shania hates mice.	Sam doesn't like TV.

Ava and Elsa love the mountains.

Cats don't like the rain.

Manuel likes his book.

🔊

40.4 ÉCRIVEZ CHAQUE PHRASE À LA FORME NÉGATIVE AVEC « DOESN'T » OU « DON'T ».

Jack likes London.	*Jack doesn't like London.*
① Imelda hates pasta.	
② My dog loves steak.	
③ Our grandfather likes coffee.	
④ I love the sea.	
⑤ Sam and Jen hate hockey.	
⑥ You like the countryside.	
⑦ We like our new cell phones.	

40.5 ÉCOUTEZ L'ENREGISTREMENT, PUIS COCHEZ LES BONNES RÉPONSES.

Anna parle de ce qu'elle aime et de ce qu'elle n'aime pas sur Radio Chat.

Anna likes Matt's...
hat ☐   glasses. ☑

① She doesn't like...
hockey ☐   golf. ☐

② Anna likes...
some actors ☐   all actors. ☐

③ She loves...
pizza ☐   pasta. ☐

④ She doesn't like...
spiders ☐   snakes. ☐

40.6 UTILISEZ LE SCHÉMA POUR CRÉER 9 PHRASES, PUIS LISEZ-LES À VOIX HAUTE.

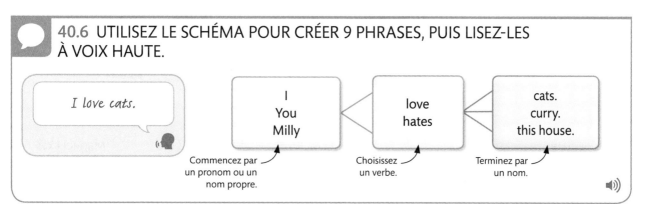

I love cats.

| I / You / Milly | love / hates | cats. / curry. / this house. |

Commencez par un pronom ou un nom propre.
Choisissez un verbe.
Terminez par un nom.

40.7 POINT CLÉ AIMER OU NE PAS AIMER AVEC LE GÉRONDIF

Vous pouvez utiliser les verbes tels que « like » et « hate »
avec des gérondifs pour parler d'activités.

They like **playing chess.**

Ed doesn't like **cycling.**

I love **swimming.**

She hates **shopping.**

40.8 AUTRES EXEMPLES AIMER OU NE PAS AIMER AVEC LE GÉRONDIF

Vi and Lu love **playing golf.**

I don't like **working late.**

Elliot loves **watching birds.**

You like **drinking coffee.**

40.9 ÉCOUTEZ L'ENREGISTREMENT, PUIS RELIEZ CHAQUE PHRASE À LA PERSONNE CORRESPONDANTE.

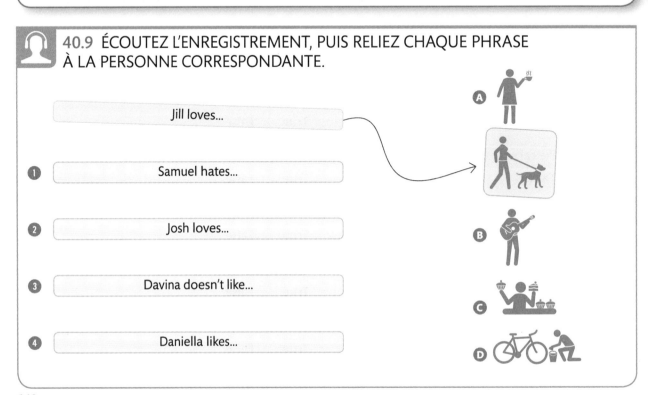

Jill loves...

❶ Samuel hates...

❷ Josh loves...

❸ Davina doesn't like...

❹ Daniella likes...

48   OLDTON NEWS

CLUBS AND SOCIETIES

An Oldton student tells us about some local clubs

I am Mark Watson and I'm at Oldton University. This is the first week of classes and students are trying lots of activities. This is what I think of them…

Chocolate Club: Do you like chocolate? Well, the people in this club love it! I don't like chocolate, so this club is not for me. They make chocolate cakes and chocolate drinks.

Dancing Club: My girlfriend loves this club. She goes twice a week. It is great exercise, but I hate it because I am very clumsy.

Computer Gaming Club: I love playing computer games at home. I really like playing with other people, too, so I like this club. There are lots of players there every week.

Chess Club: I love playing chess. I go to this club because it's a lot of fun. The players are very good, so I don't win very often. It makes me a better player.

Skateboarding Club: This is a fantastic club where you can learn from great skateboarders. This club meets three times a week and it's a great place to make new friends. I love it!

Mark loves chocolate.
True ☐   **False** ☑

❶ People make cakes at Chocolate Club.
True ☐   **False** ☐

❷ Mark's girlfriend hates dancing.
True ☐   **False** ☐

❸ Mark likes dancing.
True ☐   **False** ☐

❹ He loves computer games.
True ☐   **False** ☐

❺ He doesn't like the chess club.
True ☐   **False** ☐

❻ The players are very good.
True ☐   **False** ☐

❼ Skateboarding Club is horrible.
True ☐   **False** ☐

❽ Skateboarding Club meets three times a week.
True ☐   **False** ☐

❾ Mark loves three of the clubs.
True ☐   **False** ☐

40.11 VOCABULAIRE JUSTIFIER VOS GOÛTS

Vous pouvez employer ces adjectifs pour expliquer pourquoi vous aimez ou n'aimez pas quelque chose.

exciting

interesting

tiring

fun

delicious

disgusting

boring

40.12 POINT CLÉ LES QUESTIONS AVEC « DO » CONCERNANT LES GOÛTS

Utilisez « do » ou « does » pour demander à quelqu'un s'il aime quelque chose.

Utilisez « do » pour poser une question.

Do you like **chocolate?**

Yes, I do. It's **delicious.**

Vous pouvez utiliser « it » pour éviter la répétition du sujet.

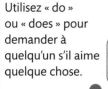

Do you like **fishing?**

No, I don't. It's **boring.**

40.13 POINT CLÉ LES QUESTIONS AVEC « WHY » CONCERNANT LES GOÛTS

Vous pouvez utiliser « why » pour connaître les raisons pour lesquelles quelqu'un aime ou n'aime pas quelque chose.

Utilisez « why » pour demander la raison.

Why do you like **basketball?**

I love **it because it's exciting.**

Vous pouvez utiliser « because » pour relier les 2 parties de votre réponse.

Why don't you like **skating?**

I hate **it because it's tiring.**

40.14 ÉCRIVEZ 7 QUESTIONS À PARTIR DES AFFIRMATIONS.

They hate football because it's boring.
Why do they hate football?

1 Una loves skiing because it's exciting.

_____

2 They like this book because it's interesting.

_____

3 Debbie doesn't like her job because it's boring.

_____

4 We don't like cooking.

_____

5 She loves surfing.

_____

6 I hate working late.

_____

7 Aziz loves Ontario.

_____

40.15 COMPLÉTEZ LES PHRASES AVEC LES MOTS DE LA LISTE, PUIS LISEZ-LES À VOIX HAUTE.

Why do they like pasta?

They like pasta because _____ *it's delicious* _____.

1 Why do you like English class?

I like English class because _____.

2 Why do you love skating?

We love skating because _____.

3 Why does Luca hate cleaning?

He hates cleaning because _____.

it's exciting

~~it's delicious~~

it's boring

it's interesting

40 ✓ CHECK-LIST

⚙ « Love », « like » et « hate » ☐   **Aa** La nourriture, les sports et les passe-temps ☐   🧩 Parler de ce que vous aimez ☐

145

41.1 LA MUSIQUE

classical music

hip-hop

jazz

country

opera

soul

rap

rock

pop

Latin

orchestra

band /group

play the trumpet

guitar player

concert

festival

sing a song

singer

headphones

album

dance

microphone

conductor

audience

guitar

electric guitar

piano

keyboard

violin

saxophone

harmonica

trumpet

drum

flute

42 Exprimer vos préférences

On utilise « like » et « love » pour indiquer à quel point on apprécie quelque chose. On utilise « favorite » pour désigner l'élément que l'on aime le plus dans un groupe.

⚙ **Grammaire** Utiliser « favorite »
Aa Vocabulaire La nourriture et la musique
🧩 **Compétence** Parler de ce que vous préférez

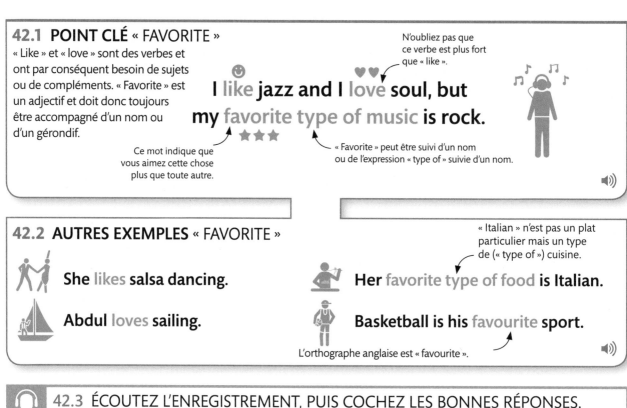

42.1 POINT CLÉ « FAVORITE »

« Like » et « love » sont des verbes et ont par conséquent besoin de sujets ou de compléments. « Favorite » est un adjectif et doit donc toujours être accompagné d'un nom ou d'un gérondif.

N'oubliez pas que ce verbe est plus fort que « like ».

I like jazz and I love soul, but my favorite type of music is rock.

Ce mot indique que vous aimez cette chose plus que toute autre.

« Favorite » peut être suivi d'un nom ou de l'expression « type of » suivie d'un nom.

42.2 AUTRES EXEMPLES « FAVORITE »

« Italian » n'est pas un plat particulier mais un type de (« type of ») cuisine.

She likes salsa dancing.

Abdul loves sailing.

Her favorite type of food is Italian.

Basketball is his favourite sport.

L'orthographe anglaise est « favourite ».

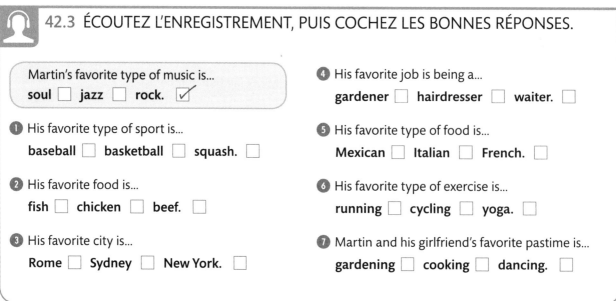

42.3 ÉCOUTEZ L'ENREGISTREMENT, PUIS COCHEZ LES BONNES RÉPONSES.

Martin's favorite type of music is...
soul ☐ **jazz** ☐ **rock.** ✓

① His favorite type of sport is...
baseball ☐ **basketball** ☐ **squash.** ☐

② His favorite food is...
fish ☐ **chicken** ☐ **beef.** ☐

③ His favorite city is...
Rome ☐ **Sydney** ☐ **New York.** ☐

④ His favorite job is being a...
gardener ☐ **hairdresser** ☐ **waiter.** ☐

⑤ His favorite type of food is...
Mexican ☐ **Italian** ☐ **French.** ☐

⑥ His favorite type of exercise is...
running ☐ **cycling** ☐ **yoga.** ☐

⑦ Martin and his girlfriend's favorite pastime is...
gardening ☐ **cooking** ☐ **dancing.** ☐

42.4 COCHEZ L'IMAGE QUI CORRESPOND À CHAQUE AFFIRMATION.

Jack's **favorite** music is jazz.

Ⓐ ☐ Ⓑ ☑ Ⓒ ☐

❸ Aman's **favorite** sport is hockey.

Ⓐ ☐ Ⓑ ☐ Ⓒ ☐

❶ Ava's **favorite** thing is her new dress.

Ⓐ ☐ Ⓑ ☐ Ⓒ ☐

❹ Mo and Jamie's **favorite** food is chocolate.

Ⓐ ☐ Ⓑ ☐ Ⓒ ☐

❷ Deborah's **favorite** pet is her dog.

Ⓐ ☐ Ⓑ ☐ Ⓒ ☐

❺ Atif's **favorite** city is New York.

Ⓐ ☐ Ⓑ ☐ Ⓒ ☐

42.5 COMPLÉTEZ LES PHRASES AVEC LES MOTS DE LA LISTE.

Dana's favorite type of music is _____opera_____.

❶ Grace's favorite food is _____.

❷ Poppy's favorite sport is _____.

❸ Dylan's favorite animal is his _____.

❹ Justin's favorite country is _____.

❺ Ling's favorite pastime is _____.

❻ Abdul's favorite color is _____.

❼ Mira's favorite number is _____.

❽ Jacob's favorite sweater is _____.

❾ Tori's favorite relative is her _____.

| surfing | ~~opera~~ | cousin | horse | pizza | 10 |
| Australia | | knitting | purple | woolen | |

🔊

42.6 ÉTUDIEZ LES PROFILS EN LIGNE SUIVANTS, COMPLÉTEZ LES PHRASES, PUIS LISEZ-LES À VOIX HAUTE.

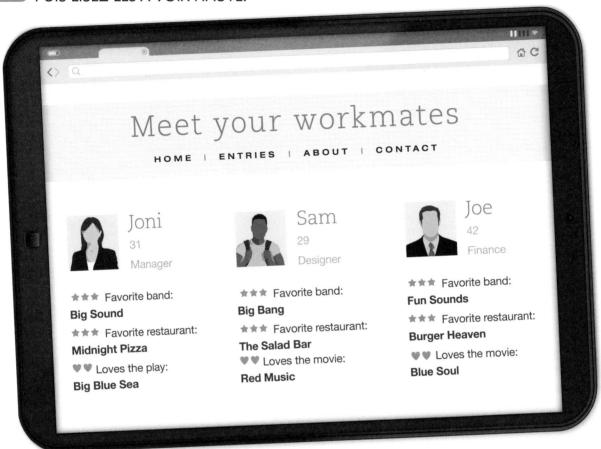

Joni's favorite band is ___Big Sound___.

1. Sam's _____ is Big Bang.

2. Joe's favorite band is _____.

3. Joni's _____ is Midnight Pizza.

4. Sam's favorite restaurant is _____.

5. Joe's _____ is Burger Heaven.

6. Joni _____ called Big Blue Sea.

7. Joe loves the movie called _____.

150

42.7 LISEZ L'ARTICLE, PUIS COCHEZ LES BONNES RÉPONSES.

> What is the favorite time to exercise?
> **morning** ☐ **afternoon** ☑ **evening** ☐

1 What type of exercise is their favorite?

yoga ☐ **running** ☐ **swimming** ☐

2 What is Stanton people's favorite type of food?

pizza ☐ **burgers** ☐ **ice cream** ☐

3 What is their favorite sport?

golf ☐ **football** ☐ **surfing** ☐

4 Their favorite night out is going to...

the movies ☐ **the theater** ☐ **a restaurant.** ☐

STANTON REVIEW

Town favorites

What's your favorite time to exercise? The morning, the afternoon, or the evening? In Stanton, people say it's the morning because there are too many other things to do in the evening. The favorite exercise is yoga: 20 classes take place each week.

Stanton townspeople like food. They eat lots of it: 4,000,000 burgers, 2,000,000 pizzas, and 3,000,000 ice cream cones every year.

And how about sports? In Stanton, there are hundreds of golfers and football players, but the favorite sport is surfing.

People like going out in the evening. Many love movies and the theater, but that's not their favorite night out. It's dinner in a restaurant. Food again. That's not a surprise!

---

42 ✓ CHECK-LIST

⚙ Utiliser « favorite » ☐   **Aa** La nourriture et la musique ☐   🧩 Parler de ce que vous préférez ☐

🔄 BILAN L'ANGLAIS QUE VOUS AVEZ APPRIS DANS LES CHAPITRES 36-42

NOUVEAU POINT LINGUISTIQUE	EXEMPLE TYPE	☑	CHAPITRE
« GO » AVEC LE GÉRONDIF, « PLAY » AVEC UN NOM	I go swimming **on Mondays** and I play tennis **with my brother on Fridays.**	☐	37.1, 37.7
LES ADVERBES DE FRÉQUENCE	I always watch TV **at night,** and I sometimes go the the movies.	☐	39.1
LES QUESTIONS SUR LE TEMPS LIBRE	How often do you **go on vacation?** When does she **go running?**	☐	39.6
EXPRIMER DES GOÛTS	She likes **tennis.** Max doesn't like **pizza.** I love **swimming.** She hates **shopping.**	☐	40.1, 40.7
LES QUESTIONS SUR LES GOÛTS	Do you like **chocolate?** Why do you like **basketball?**	☐	40.12, 40.13
« FAVORITE »	My favorite type of **music is rock.**	☐	42.1

43 Vocabulaire

43.1 LES COMPÉTENCES

jump

climb

fly

ride

drive

play

kick

throw

hit

catch

see

listen

whisper

talk

speak

shout

carry

make (a snowman)

do (homework)

think

act

remember

understand

spell

sit

stand up

walk

move

lift

work

add

subtract

44 Ce que vous pouvez ou ne pouvez pas faire

Utilisez « can » pour parler de choses que vous êtes capable de faire, comme faire du vélo ou jouer de la guitare. Utilisez « cannot » ou « can't » pour parler de ce que vous ne pouvez pas faire.

⚙ **Grammaire** « Can », « cannot » et « can't »
Aa Vocabulaire Les talents et les compétences
🧩 **Compétence** Dire ce que vous pouvez ou ne pouvez pas faire

44.1 POINT CLÉ « CAN », « CANNOT » ET CAN'T »

« Can » se place entre le sujet et le verbe. Après « can », on ne met que le radical du verbe (l'infinitif sans « to »).

À NOTER
La forme négative longue « cannot » s'écrit toujours en un mot et non deux.

I can ride a bicycle.
Radical du verbe.

He can play the guitar.
« Can » est toujours conjugué de la même manière. Il ne se modifie pas en fonction du sujet.

I {cannot / can't} sing jazz songs.
Forme contractée de « cannot ».

44.2 AUTRES EXEMPLES « CAN », « CANNOT » ET CAN'T »

 Janet can play tennis.

 He cannot climb the tree.

 Bob can swim well.

 **They can't lift the box.**

44.3 CONSTRUCTION « CAN », « CANNOT » ET CAN'T »

SUJET	CAN/CANNOT/CAN'T	RADICAL	COMPLÉMENT
She	can / cannot / can't	ride	a bicycle.

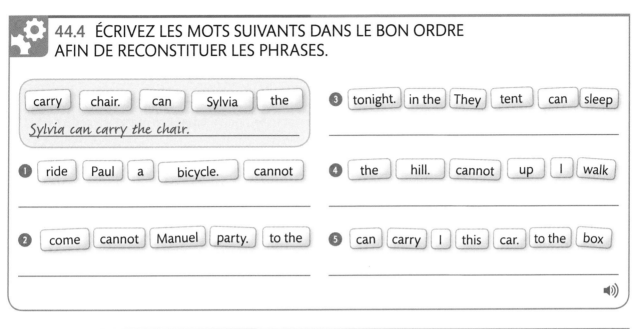

44.4 ÉCRIVEZ LES MOTS SUIVANTS DANS LE BON ORDRE AFIN DE RECONSTITUER LES PHRASES.

carry chair. can Sylvia the

Sylvia can carry the chair.

1 ride Paul a bicycle. cannot

_____

2 come cannot Manuel party. to the

_____

3 tonight. in the They tent can sleep

_____

4 the hill. cannot up I walk

_____

5 can carry I this car. to the box

_____

44.5 BARREZ LE MOT INCORRECT DANS CHAQUE PHRASE.

My son is sick. He ~~can~~ / can't go to school today.

1 Jo's pen doesn't work. She can / can't write her letter.

2 I understand the homework, so I can / can't do it.

3 The museum is closed. We can / can't get in.

4 I have the car today, so I can / can't drive you.

5 It's cold outside, so we can / can't have a picnic.

6 Tony needs to work late, so he can / can't come.

7 We can / can't play tennis. It's too dark.

44.6 RÉCRIVEZ LA PHRASE À LA FORME AFFIMATIVE OU NÉGATIVE, COMME DANS L'EXEMPLE.

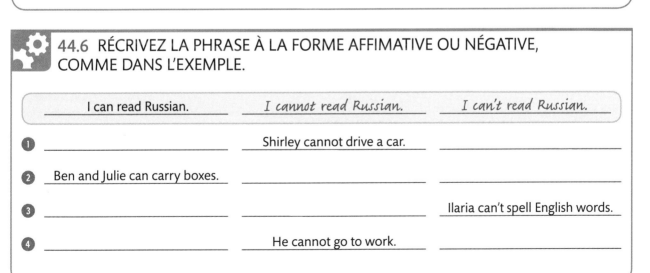

I can read Russian.	I cannot read Russian.	I can't read Russian.
1	Shirley cannot drive a car.	
2 Ben and Julie can carry boxes.		
3		Ilaria can't spell English words.
4	He cannot go to work.	

44.7 POINT CLÉ LES QUESTIONS ET LES RÉPONSES COURTES

Pour poser une question avec « can », placez « can » devant le sujet. Lorsque vous répondez à une question avec « can », vous n'êtes pas obligé de répéter tous les mots de la question.

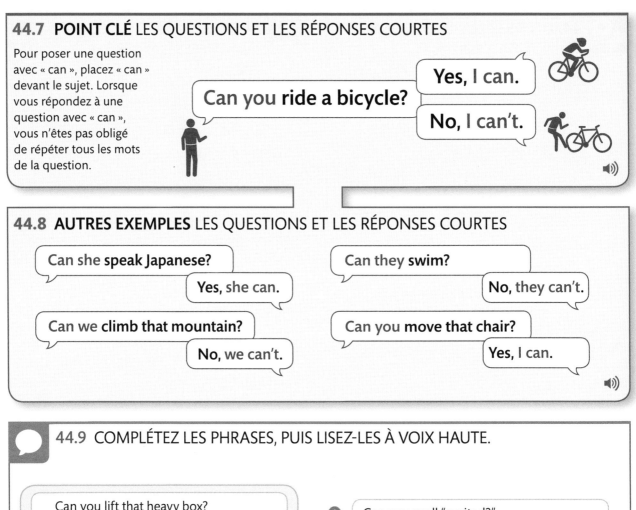

Can you **ride a bicycle?**

Yes, I can.

No, I can't.

44.8 AUTRES EXEMPLES LES QUESTIONS ET LES RÉPONSES COURTES

Can she **speak Japanese?**

Yes, she can.

Can we **climb that mountain?**

No, we can't.

Can they **swim?**

No, they can't.

Can you **move that chair?**

Yes, I can.

44.9 COMPLÉTEZ LES PHRASES, PUIS LISEZ-LES À VOIX HAUTE.

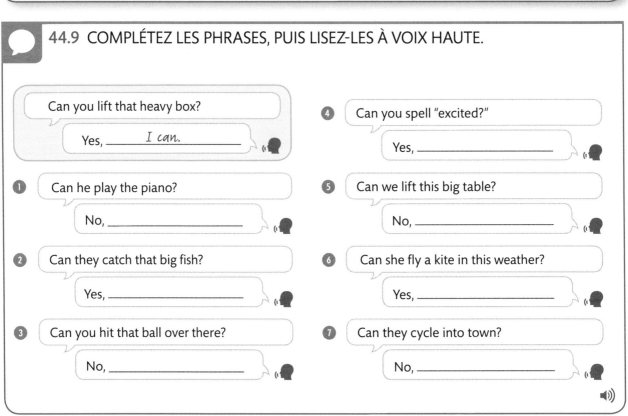

Can you lift that heavy box?

Yes, _____*I can.*_____

1 Can he play the piano?

No, _____

2 Can they catch that big fish?

Yes, _____

3 Can you hit that ball over there?

No, _____

4 Can you spell "excited?"

Yes, _____

5 Can we lift this big table?

No, _____

6 Can she fly a kite in this weather?

Yes, _____

7 Can they cycle into town?

No, _____

44.10 POSEZ LES QUESTIONS CORRESPONDANT AUX AFFIRMATIONS SUIVANTES.

Paul and Mary can speak Chinese.
Can Paul and Mary speak Chinese?

❶ The dog can jump over the wall.
_____

❷ Denise can touch her toes.
_____

❸ I can lift my son onto my shoulders.
_____

❹ Grandma can see the TV.
_____

❺ I can hit the tennis ball over the net.
_____

🔊

44.11 ÉCOUTEZ, PUIS COCHEZ LES BONNES RÉPONSES.

Sheila et Mark parlent de ce qu'ils peuvent et ne peuvent pas cuisiner.

Sheila can make a salad.
True ✓ **False** ☐

❶ Sheila doesn't eat meat.
True ☐ **False** ☐

❷ Mark can't cook a roast chicken.
True ☐ **False** ☐

❸ Sheila and Mark can both cook vegetables.
True ☐ **False** ☐

❹ Sheila can make an apple pie.
True ☐ **False** ☐

44.12 COMPLÉTEZ LES PHRASES AVEC « CAN » OU « CANNOT ».

Janet is a chef. She _____ *can* _____ cook very well.

❶ Paul and Jerry don't like the ocean because they _____ swim.

❷ I ride my bike to work because I _____ drive.

❸ Jim cannot climb over the wall, but he _____ walk around it.

❹ My mother _____ lift that bag because it's too heavy.

❺ My sister Penny loves music and _____ dance to any song.

🔊

44 ✓ CHECK-LIST

⚙ « Can », « cannot » et « can't » ☐   **Aa** Les talents et les compétences ☐   🧩 Dire ce que vous pouvez ou ne pouvez pas faire ☐

45 Décrire vos actions

Les mots « quietly » et « loudly » sont des adverbes.
Ils permettent de donner plus d'informations concernant
le verbe. Vous pouvez donc les utiliser pour décrire
la façon dont vous faites quelque chose.

⚙ **Grammaire** Les adverbes réguliers et irréguliers
Aa Vocabulaire Les loisirs et les activités
🧩 **Compétence** Décrire des activités

45.1 POINT CLÉ LES ADVERBES

Les adverbes se placent
généralement après le verbe
qu'ils décrivent.

« Quietly » décrit la manière
dont je parle.

I speak quietly.

He speaks loudly.

« Loudly » décrit la manière
dont il parle.

Hello.

HELLO!

45.2 AUTRES EXEMPLES LES ADVERBES

A tortoise moves slowly.

Horses can run quickly.

She sings beautifully.

I can play the piano badly.

45.3 COMPLÉTEZ LES PHRASES AVEC LES MOTS DE LA LISTE.

Tommy plays the guitar ___*badly*___.

 3 The old man walks _____.

1 Mary can speak French _____.

4 He talks very _____.

2 Roger can run very _____.

5 She won the race _____.

| excellently | ~~badly~~ | loudly | quickly | easily | slowly |

45.4 POINT CLÉ LES ADVERBES RÉGULIERS ET IRRÉGULIERS

ADVERBES RÉGULIERS

Pour former la plupart des adverbes, il suffit d'ajouter « -ly » à l'adjectif. Si l'adjectif se termine en « -y », ôtez le « -y » et ajoutez « -ily ».

bad → **badly**

careful → **carefully**

easy → **easily**

Ôtez le « -y » et ajoutez « -ily ».

ADVERBES IRRÉGULIERS

Certains adverbes sont totalement différents de l'adjectif. D'autres sont identiques. Ces adverbes sont dits irréguliers.

good → **well**

L'adverbe est totalement différent de l'adjectif.

hard → **hard**

L'adverbe est identique à l'adjectif.

early → **early**

Les adjectifs se terminant en « -ly » ne changent pas.

Aa 45.5 ENTOUREZ 8 ADVERBES, PUIS CLASSEZ-LES.

```
E A S I L Y W L K Q G
B N O Y U T E O A U R
A J S L O X L S G I W
D F L O U D L Y T C E
L F H A B L W H F K M
Y A G A R U E A R L Y
C S F U S Y Q R V Y W
I T R S L K A D B M S
```

RÉGULIERS

1. Loudly
2. _____
3. _____
4. _____

IRRÉGULIERS

5. Fast
6. _____
7. _____
8. _____

45.6 RÉCRIVEZ LES PHRASES EN CORRIGEANT LES ERREURS.

My friend John walks very quick.
My friend John walks very quickly.

1. You speak English very good.

_____

2. Damian cooks burgers bad.

_____

3. I can get to your house easy.

_____

4. Benjy always listens careful.

_____

5. My brother always works hardly.

_____

6. Sammy always plays his guitar loud.

_____

45.7 DIRE AUTREMENT VOUS FAITES QUELQUE CHOSE BIEN

Utilisez un gérondif ou un nom après l'expression « good at » pour dire ce que vous faites bien.

She can run well.

She's good at running.

Vous pouvez utiliser le gérondif après « good at ».

45.8 CONSTRUCTION « GOOD AT » ET « BAD AT »

Le contraire de « good at » est « bad at ».

SUJET + VERBE	« GOOD AT » OU « BAD AT »	GÉRONDIF OU NOM
She's	good at bad at	skiing. English.

45.9 AUTRES EXEMPLES « GOOD AT » ET « BAD AT »

 Aziz is good at climbing trees.

 I am bad at making cakes.

 Kate is good at soccer.

 Harris is bad at chess.

 45.10 ÉCRIVEZ LES MOTS SUIVANTS DANS LE BON ORDRE AFIN DE RECONSTITUER LES PHRASES.

the guitar. | good at | playing | Pablo is

Pablo is good at playing the guitar.

③ writing | Mary is | bad at | German.

_____

① is | at | good | My horse | jumping.

_____

④ good | swimming. | at | are | Jo and Bob

_____

② bad at | early. | getting up | I am

_____

⑤ cleaning. | is | Millie | bad at

_____

160

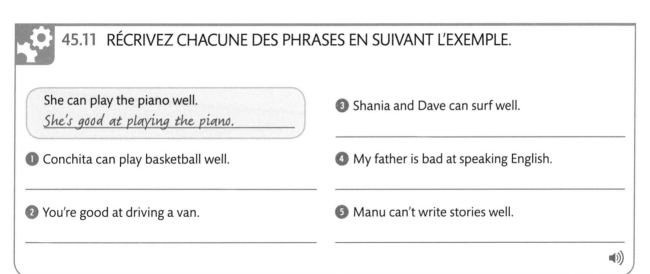

45.11 RÉCRIVEZ CHACUNE DES PHRASES EN SUIVANT L'EXEMPLE.

> She can play the piano well.
> *She's good at playing the piano.*

1 Conchita can play basketball well.

_____

2 You're good at driving a van.

_____

3 Shania and Dave can surf well.

_____

4 My father is bad at speaking English.

_____

5 Manu can't write stories well.

_____

45.12 BON OU PAS ? ÉCOUTEZ, PUIS COCHEZ LA BONNE RÉPONSE.

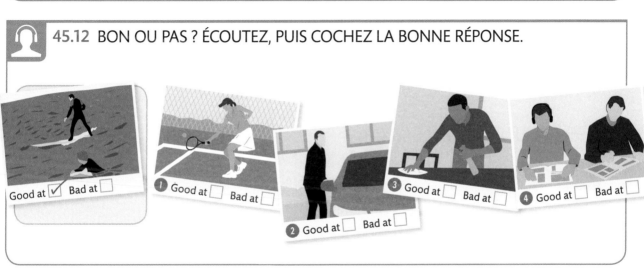

Good at ✔ Bad at ☐

1 Good at ☐ Bad at ☐

2 Good at ☐ Bad at ☐

3 Good at ☐ Bad at ☐

4 Good at ☐ Bad at ☐

45.13 UTILISEZ LE SCHÉMA POUR CRÉER 12 PHRASES, PUIS LISEZ-LES À VOIX HAUTE.

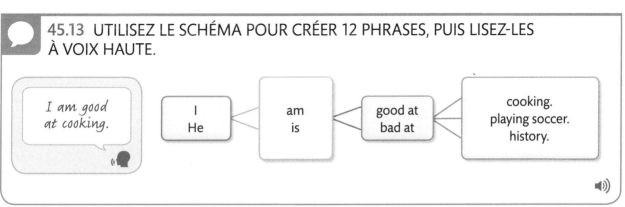

> *I am good at cooking.*

| I / He | am / is | good at / bad at | cooking. / playing soccer. / history. |

45 ✓ CHECK-LIST

Les adverbes réguliers et irréguliers ☐   **Aa** Les loisirs et les activités ☐   Décrire des activités ☐

46 Décrire vos compétences

Les mots « quite » et « very » sont des adverbes modificateurs. Vous pouvez les utiliser devant d'autres adverbes pour préciser la façon dont vous faites quelque chose.

⚙ **Grammaire** Les adverbes modificateurs
Aa Vocabulaire Les aptitudes et compétences
🧩 **Compétence** Parler de ce que vous faites bien

46.1 POINT CLÉ LES ADVERBES MODIFICATEURS

Si vous faites quelque chose « quite well », vous êtes bon mais pas excellent. Si vous le faites « very » ou « really well », vous êtes excellent.

« Quite » modifie l'adverbe principal « well » et celui-ci se place devant.

CONSEIL
En américain, on utilise « quite » pour amplifier l'adverbe.

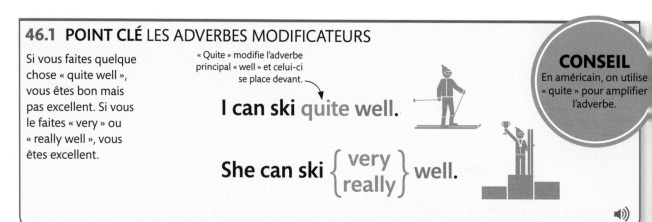

I can ski quite well.

She can ski { very / really } well.

46.2 AUTRES EXEMPLES LES ADVERBES MODIFICATEURS

 Ben can climb really high.

 My dad dances quite well.

 Jenny can swim very well.

 I speak Spanish quite well.

Aa 46.3 RELIEZ LE DÉBUT DE CHAQUE PHRASE À LA FIN QUI LUI CORRESPOND.

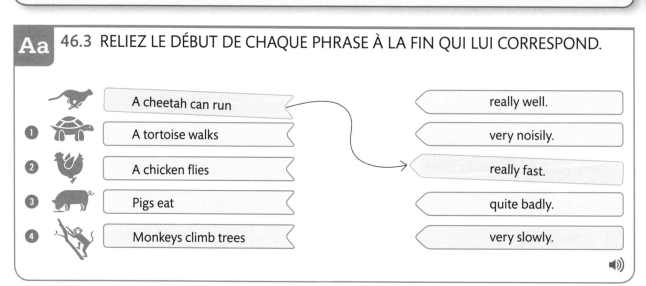

A cheetah can run — really fast.

1. A tortoise walks — very noisily.

2. A chicken flies — really well.

3. Pigs eat — quite badly.

4. Monkeys climb trees — very slowly.

46.4 POINT CLÉ LES ADVERBES MODIFICATEURS AVEC « GOOD AT »

Vous pouvez également utiliser les adverbes modificateurs avec les expressions « good at » et « bad at ».

She can play golf quite well.

She's quite good at **playing golf.**

« Quite » modifie « good at ».

N'oubliez pas que « good at » et « bad at » sont suivis par un gérondif.

You can play golf { very / really } **well.**

You're { very / really } **good at playing golf.**

« Very » et « really » se placent devant « good at ».

46.5 LISEZ LE RAPPORT, PUIS COCHEZ LES BONNES RÉPONSES.

English report: Juan Ramirez

Writing 99%	Excellent.
Vocabulary 65%	Ok, but you need to study more.
Speaking 95%	Well done.
Listening 66%	Better. Try watching more English movies to improve.
Reading 63%	Ok. You need to read more English texts to improve.

How good is Juan at learning vocabulary?
Quite good ✓ **Really good** ☐

❶ How good is he at speaking English?
Quite good ☐ **Really good** ☐

❷ How good is Juan at reading?
Quite good ☐ **Really good** ☐

❸ How good is he at listening to English?
Quite good ☐ **Really good** ☐

❹ How good is Juan at writing English?
Quite good ☐ **Really good** ☐

---

46 ✓ CHECK-LIST

⚙ Les adverbes modificateurs ☐   **Aa** Les aptitudes et les compétences ☐   Parler de ce que vous faites bien ☐

Exprimer vos souhaits

Vous pouvez utiliser « I want » et « I would like » pour indiquer ce que vous voulez faire. Vous pouvez aussi les utiliser à la forme négative pour dire ce que vous ne désirez pas faire.

⚙ **Grammaire**   « Would » et « want »
Aa Vocabulaire   Les activités de loisir
🧩 **Compétence** Parler de vos ambitions

47.1 POINT CLÉ « I WOULD LIKE » ET « I WANT »

« I would like » et « I want » permettent d'exprimer un souhait, mais « I want » est plus fort.

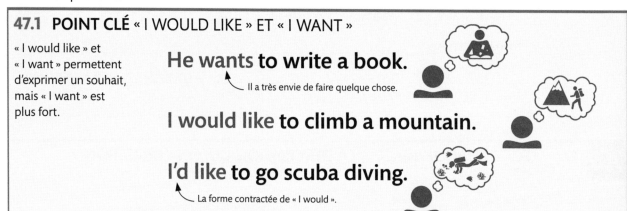

He wants to write a book.

Il a très envie de faire quelque chose.

I would like to climb a mountain.

I'd like to go scuba diving.

La forme contractée de « I would ».

47.2 CONSTRUCTION « I WOULD LIKE » ET « I WANT »

« Would » est un verbe modal, donc il ne change pas de forme.

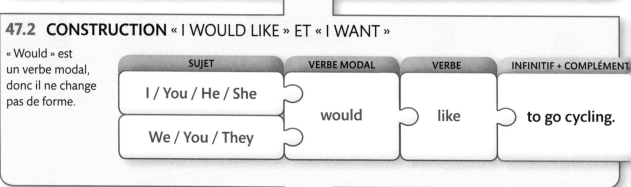

SUJET	VERBE MODAL	VERBE	INFINITIF + COMPLÉMENT
I / You / He / She	would	like	to go cycling.
We / You / They			

47.3 AUTRES EXEMPLES « I'D LIKE » ET « I WANT »

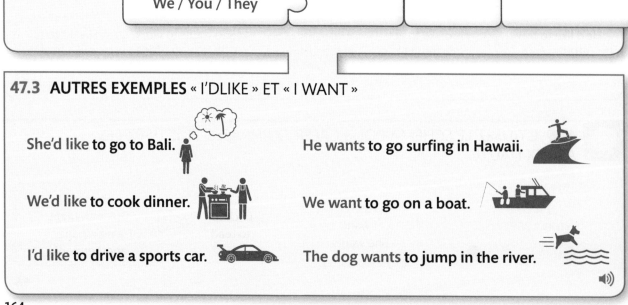

She'd like to go to Bali.

He wants to go surfing in Hawaii.

We'd like to cook dinner.

We want to go on a boat.

I'd like to drive a sports car.

The dog wants to jump in the river.

47.4 RÉCRIVEZ LA PHRASE DE 2 MANIÈRES DIFFÉRENTES.

I want to buy a house.	*I would like to buy a house.*	*I'd like to buy a house.*
❶ _____	_____	He'd like to get a dog.
❷ _____	You would like to work in Turkey.	_____
❸ We want to learn Chinese.	_____	_____
❹ _____	_____	They'd like to start a rock band.

Aa 47.5 RELIEZ CHAQUE IMAGE À LA DESCRIPTION QUI LUI CORRESPOND.

| He'd like to travel around Asia. | He'd like to act in a musical. | He wants to be in the Olympics. | She wants to work with lions in Africa. | She'd like to sail a boat. |

47.6 UTILISEZ LE SCHÉMA POUR CRÉER 12 PHRASES, PUIS LISEZ-LES À VOIX HAUTE.

I'd like to climb this tree.

I'd like		this tree.
I want	to climb	that mountain.
She wants	to read	a newspaper.
		another book.

47.7 POINT CLÉ LES FORMES NÉGATIVES DE « I WOULD LIKE » ET « I WANT »

Utilisez « not » après « would » pour former la forme négative. « Don't » et « doesn't » se placent devant « want ».

I would not like to go snowboarding.

I wouldn't like to go shopping.

La forme contractée de « would not ».

They don't want to go fishing.

« Don't » se place devant « want ».

47.8 AUTRES EXEMPLES LES FORMES NÉGATIVES « I WOULD LIKE » ET « I WANT »

They wouldn't like to go swimming.

We don't want to eat dinner.

She wouldn't like to be a hairdresser.

He doesn't want to go shopping.

47.9 RÉCRIVEZ LA PHRASE DE 2 MANIÈRES DIFFÉRENTES.

I would not like to go skiing.	I wouldn't like to go skiing.	I don't want to go skiing.
❶ _____	_____	He doesn't want to play tennis.
❷ _____	She wouldn't like to study science.	_____
❸ _____	_____	They don't want to go to work.
❹ You would not like to sing.	_____	_____
❺ _____	We wouldn't like to go diving.	_____

47.10 POINT CLÉ LES QUESTIONS ET LES RÉPONSES COURTES

Dans une question, « would » se place devant le sujet.

Would you like to play chess? **Yes, I would.**

Does he want to go to the movies? **Yes, he does.**

« Does » se place devant le sujet dans les questions avec « want ».

47.11 ÉCOUTEZ L'ENREGISTREMENT, PUIS COCHEZ LES BONNES RÉPONSES.

Does Mark want to play tennis later?
Yes, he does. ☑   **No, he doesn't.** ☐

3 Would Lee like to work on Saturday?
Yes, he would. ☐   **No, he wouldn't.** ☐

1 Would Sarah like to go to a restaurant today?
Yes, she would. ☐   **No, she wouldn't.** ☐

4 Does Mary want to skateboard tonight?
Yes, she does. ☐   **No, she doesn't.** ☐

2 Does Vangelis want to make the dinner?
Yes, he does. ☐   **No, he doesn't.** ☐

5 Would Anoushka like to go bowling?
Yes, she would. ☐   **No, she wouldn't.** ☐

47.12 RÉCRIVEZ LES PHRASES SUIVANTES EN CORRIGEANT LES ERREURS.

Would you **want** to go home?
Would you like to go home?

3 They **doesn't** want to go to work today.
_____

1 He **don't** want to climb that hill.
_____

4 She would **want** to play tennis tonight.
_____

2 I wouldn't **likes** to be a judge.
_____

5 I **wants** to climb that tree.
_____

---

48 Parler de vos études

Lorsque vous évoquez vos études, vous pouvez utiliser « I would » et « I want » pour parler des sujets que vous voudriez apprendre. Utilisez les adverbes pour dire à quel point vous souhaitez les étudier.

⚙ **Grammaire** Les adverbes et les articles
Aa Vocabulaire Les matières scolaires
🧩 **Compétence** Parler de vos ambitions

48.1 VOCABULAIRE LES MATIÈRES SCOLAIRES

 art and design

 drama

 physical education

 English

 music

 math (US) maths (UK)

 science

 chemistry

 biology

 physics

 geography

 history

48.2 POINT CLÉ « REALLY » ET « QUITE »

L'adverbe « really » signifie que vous voulez réellement faire quelque chose. « Quite » est moins fort.

I love music. I'd really like to study it next term.

Votre désir de faire ceci est très fort.

I like biology. I'd quite like to study it next year.

Votre désir n'est pas si fort.

48.3 AUTRES EXEMPLES « REALLY » ET « QUITE »

Bella is good at science, and she'd really like to study it at college.

Richard loves jazz, so he'd really like to go to that music festival.

This band is OK. I'd quite like to listen to their new CD.

48.4 VOCABULAIRE ÉTUDIER

 learn

 practice (US) practise (UK)

 take an exam

 pass an exam

get a degree

48.5 ÉCRIVEZ LES MOTS SUIVANTS DANS LE BON ORDRE AFIN DE RECONSTITUER LES PHRASES.

to do | quite | an English degree. | like | Sheila | would

Sheila would quite like to do an English degree.

① his driving test. | Jerry | really | would | to pass | like

_____

② would | an IELTS test. | like | Ben and Sam | to take | really

_____

③ like | Helen | her English. | would | to practice | quite

_____

④ the piano | like | quite | to play | tonight. | I'd

_____

48.6 UTILISEZ LE SCHÉMA POUR CRÉER 12 PHRASES, PUIS LISEZ-LES À VOIX HAUTE.

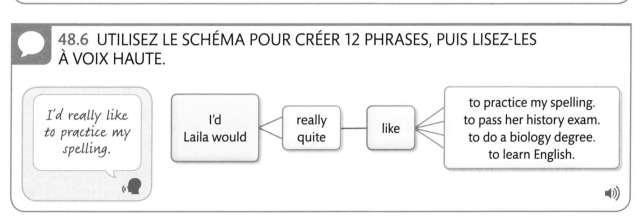

I'd really like to practice my spelling.

I'd
Laila would — really quite — like — to practice my spelling.
to pass her history exam.
to do a biology degree.
to learn English.

169

48.7 POINT CLÉ L'ARTICLE ZÉRO

On n'utilise pas d'article (« a » ou « the ») avec certains lieux et certaines institutions lorsqu'on explique leur fonction.

Elle va là pour étudier, ce qui est l'objectif de l'école en général. On n'utilise donc pas d'article.

Liz is seven. She goes to school now.

Larry works at the school in Park Street.

Utilisez l'article pour parler du bâtiment précis où il travaille.

48.8 AUTRES EXEMPLES L'ARTICLE ZÉRO

ARTICLE ZÉRO	ARTICLE
I am at university in Chicago.	**The University of Chicago is good.**
Pierre is in hospital.	**The hospital is far away.**
Liz goes to church on Sundays.	**St. Mary's is an old church.**
Go to bed, Tom!	**Your shirt is on the bed.**
Sue is in town this afternoon.	**Hancock is a nice town.**
Sarah studies at home.	**This dog hasn't got a home.**

48.9 BARREZ LE MOT INCORRECT DANS CHAQUE PHRASE.

Sheila works at ~~school~~ / the school near here.

1 Emily has **lovely home** / a lovely home.

2 Sue always takes her lunch to **office** / the office.

3 Can you see where **church** / the church is?

4 Jim went to **bed** / the bed hours ago.

5 Can you drive me into **town** / a town later?

6 I live next to **university** / the university.

7 I leave **home** / a home at 8am every weekday.

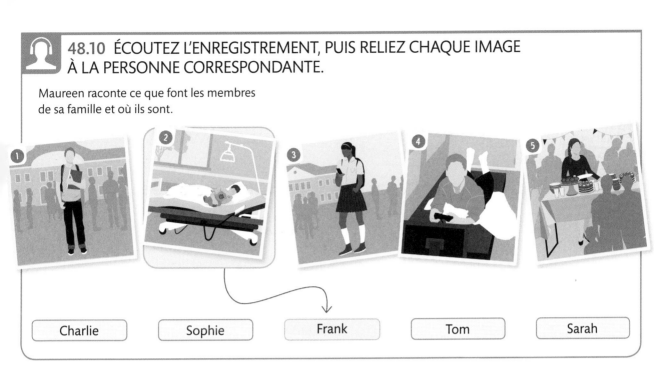

48.10 ÉCOUTEZ L'ENREGISTREMENT, PUIS RELIEZ CHAQUE IMAGE À LA PERSONNE CORRESPONDANTE.

Maureen raconte ce que font les membres de sa famille et où ils sont.

Charlie | Sophie | Frank | Tom | Sarah

48 ✓ **CHECK-LIST**

⚙ Les adverbes et articles ☐   **Aa** Les matières scolaires ☐   🧩 Parler de vos ambitions ☐

♻ BILAN L'ANGLAIS QUE VOUS AVEZ APPRIS DANS LES CHAPITRES 44-48

NOUVEAU POINT LINGUISTIQUE	EXEMPLE TYPE	☑	CHAPITRE
« CAN », « CANNOT » ET « CAN'T »	I can **ride a bicycle.** He can **play guitar.** I cannot / can't **sing jazz songs.**	☐	44.1, 44.3, 44.7
LES ADVERBES	I speak quietly. **He speaks** loudly.	☐	45.1, 45.4
« GOOD AT » ET « BAD AT »	She's good at **running.** I am bad at **making cakes.**	☐	45.7, 45.8
LES ADVERBES MODIFICATEURS	I can ski quite **well.** She can ski very **well.** She can ski really **well.**	☐	46.1, 46.4
« I WOULD LIKE » ET « I WANT »	He wants **to write a book.** I would like **to climb a mountain.**	☐	47.1, 47.7
« REALLY » ET « QUITE »	I love music. I'd really **like to study it this term.** I like biology. I'd quite **like to study it next year.**	☐	48.2, 48.3
L'ARTICLE ZÉRO	My daughter goes to school **now.**	☐	48.7, 48.8

Réponses

1.4 🔊
1. I'm Charlotte.
2. My name's Una.
3. My name's Simone.
4. I'm Carlos.
5. I'm Juan.
6. My name's Miriam.
7. I'm Sarah.

1.5
A. 5
B. 1
C. 2
D. 3
E. 6
F. 4

1.6 🔊
1. Hi! My name is Linda.
2. Hi! My name is Abdul.
3. Hi! My name is Paolo.
4. Hello! My name is Linda.
5. Hello! My name is Abdul.
6. Hello! My name is Paolo.
7. Hi! I am Linda.
8. Hi! I am Abdul.
9. Hi! I am Paolo.
10. Hello! I am Linda.
11. Hello! I am Abdul.
12. Hello! I am Paolo.

1.9
1. B-E-L-I-N-D-A
2. L-E-W-I-S
3. A-D-A-M-S
4. B-O-B
5. S-P-E-N-C-E-R
6. K-A-T-E W-A-L-L-A-C-E
7. S-A-U-L J-A-C-K-S-O-N
8. N-A-T-A-L-I-E L-A-U
9. C-H-R-I-S B-O-Y-L-E

1.10 🔊
1. B-A-S-H-I-R
2. B-E-N J-A-M-E-S
3. M-O-L-L-Y
4. L-O-P-E-Z
5. N-A-D-I-Y-A L-A-T-I-F

3.5 🔊
1. eleven
2. seventeen
3. thirty-four
4. fifty-nine
5. eighty-five

3.6 🔊
1. Theo **is** 45 years old.
2. Madison **is** 27 years old.
3. Jeremy and Tanya **are** 90 years old.
4. We **are** 29 years old.
5. I **am** 34 years old.

3.8
1. 40
2. 30
3. 19
4. 60
5. 80
6. 17
7. 13

3.12
1. Japan
2. US
3. France

3.13 🔊
1. Spanish
2. German
3. Canadian
4. American
5. Australian
6. Chinese

3.14 🔊
1. I am Australian.
2. I am English.
3. I am from Italy.
4. I am from France.
5. You are Australian.
6. You are English.
7. You are from Italy.
8. You are from France.
9. They are Australian.
10. They are English.
11. They are from Italy.
12. They are from France.

5.3 🔊
1. your horse
2. their sheep
3. our fish

4. its bone
5. his dog

5.4 🔊
1. Bingo is **my** dog.
2. **Her** aunt is called Goldie.
3. **My** cat eats fish.
4. **Their** rabbit lives in the backyard.
5. **Our** parrot is from Colombia.
6. **His** wife is called Henrietta.
7. **Their** dog is 10 years old.
8. **Our** aunt lives on a farm in Ohio.
9. Here is **its** ball.

5.5 🔊
1. Farida **is** their sister.
2. Duke **is** our dog.
3. Daisy **is** her mother.
4. They **are** his grandparents.
5. It **is** our horse.
6. John **is** our cousin.
7. I **am** Daisy's daughter.
8. You **are** my friend.

5.8 🔊
1. **This** is her horse.
2. **That** is our rabbit.
3. **That** is their pig.
4. **This** is his cow.
5. **This** is your fish.

5.9 🔊
1. Lily is their sister.
2. Our son is 12 years old.
3. That is their cow.
4. This is your ball.
5. Her father is called Caspar.

5.10
A. 2
B. 1
C. 5
D. 3
E. 4

5.11 🔊
1. This is my cat.
2. This is my parrot.
3. This is her cat.
4. This is her parrot.
5. This is their cat.
6. This is their parrot.
7. That is my cat.
8. That is my parrot.
9. That is her cat.
10. That is her parrot.
11. That is their cat.
12. That is their parrot.

6.3 🔊
1 Ben's son
2 Sam and Ayshah's cat
3 Debbie's house
4 Marco and Kate's car
5 Elsa's grandchild
6 Beth's parrot

6.4
1 Lucas is Ben's father.
2 Lily is Ben's mother.
3 Noah is Ben's son.
4 Grace is Ben's sister.
5 Alex is Ben's brother.

6.7 🔊
1 Angela is Skanda's wife.
2 That is my cousins' snake.
3 Sue is Ella and Mark's aunt.
4 Ginger is John's cat.

6.8 🔊
1 Kathy is **Dave's** aunt.
2 Rex is **Noah and Pat's** dog.
3 This is **her cousins'** house.
4 Felix is **the children's** cat.

8.2 🔊
1 **These** are Diego's keys.
2 **This** is Olivia's purse.
3 **Those** are my books.
4 **These** are my pencils.
5 **That** is Anna's sandwich.
6 **That** is Malik's phone.

8.3
1 That is his apple.
2 Those are her pens.
3 That is my ring.
4 These are our keys.
5 That is his brother.
6 These are my pencils.

8.5 🔊

8.6 🔊
1 watches
2 books
3 sandwiches
4 toothbrushes
5 necklaces
6 apples
7 keys
8 cell phones

8.9
1 This is her laptop. This laptop is hers.
2 Those are their keys. Those keys are theirs.
3 These are our passports. These passports are ours.
4 That is his brush. That brush is his.

8.10
LE SAC DE TOM:
sandwiches, cell phone, ID card, chocolate bar.
LE SAC DE SARAH:
purse, books, brush, notebook.

8.11 🔊
1. Those are my books.
2. Those are my dogs.
3. That is my brother.
4. These are my books.
5. These are my dogs.
6. This is my brother.
7. Those are Bruno's books.
8. Those are Bruno's dogs.
9. That is Bruno's brother.
10. These are Bruno's books.
11. These are Bruno's dogs.
12. This is Bruno's brother.

10.2 🔊
1 You **are a** doctor.
2 She **is a** farmer.
3 They **are** teachers.
4 We **are** nurses.
5 I **am an** actor.
6 She **is a** chef.

10.3 🔊
1 You **are** a driver.
2 I **am** a mechanic.
3 He **is** a vet.
4 We **are** sales assistants.
5 They **are** businesswomen.
6 She **is** a waitress.
7 We **are** receptionists.
8 She **is** a gardener.

10.5 🔊
1 hospital
2 farm
3 laboratory
4 restaurant
5 school
6 construction site
7 hospital
8 theater
9 restaurant

10.7
1 False 2 False 3 True 4 True

10.9
A 3
B 4
C 1
D 6
E 5
F 2

10.10 🔊
1 She **is a builder. She works on a construction site.**
2 We **are scientists. We work in a laboratory.**
3 You **are an actor. You work in a theater.**
4 He **is a waiter. He works in a restaurant.**
5 Chloe **is a nurse. She works in a hospital.**

10.13
1 Noah's mother
2 Noah's sister
3 Noah's father
4 Noah's brother

10.14 🔊
1 Selma **is a** chef. **She works with** food.
2 Max **is a** nurse. **He works with** patients.
3 Mat **is a** mechanic. **He works with** cars.
4 Ana **is a** vet. **She works with** animals.
5 Jazmin **is a** judge. **She works with** people.

11.3 🔊
1 It's midnight.
2 It's half past three.
3 It's quarter to twelve.
4 It's two thirty.
5 It's a quarter past nine.
6 It's ten thirty.

11.4
1 11:30
2 7:00
3 4:15
4 9:30
5 2:15

11.5
1. 9:00
2. 1:15
3. 3:25
4. 2:30
5. 12:15

11.6
1. It's half past five. / It's five thirty.
2. It's a quarter to seven. / It's six forty-five.
3. It's twenty-five to twelve. / It's eleven thirty-five.
4. It's a quarter past eight. / It's eight fifteen.
5. It's twenty-two past ten. / It's ten twenty-two.

13

13.4
1. He **wakes** up at 7 o'clock.
2. You **leave** home at 8:30am.
3. I **start** work at 10am.
4. Ellen **gets** up at 5 o'clock.
5. My wife **takes** a shower in the evening.
6. I **take** a shower in the morning.
7. My parents **eat** lunch at 2pm.
8. We **leave** work at 4pm.
9. My brother **works** with animals.

13.5
1. I **leave** work at 5:30pm.
2. Phil **eats** lunch at 12:30pm.
3. We **get** up at 8am.
4. His son **starts** work at 5am.
5. My sister **leaves** work at 7pm.
6. They **eat** dinner at 10pm.

13.6
1. My son **wakes** up at 5am.
2. I **leave** work at 6:30pm.
3. We **eat** breakfast at 8am.
4. Paula **works** outside.
5. My wife **starts** work at 7am.
6. He **eats** lunch at noon.

13.9
1. washes
2. watches
3. wakes
4. goes
5. finishes
6. leaves

13.10
1. Lucia **wakes** up at 7am.
2. I **get** up at 7:30am.
3. Ethan **goes** to work at 5am.
4. You **leave** work at 5pm.
5. Shona **watches** TV in the evening.

13.11
1. My mother **watches** TV in the morning.
2. We **go** to bed at midnight.
3. My husband **finishes** work at 6:30pm.
4. Rob **goes** to work at 8:30am.
5. I **take** a shower in the morning.
6. I **leave** work at 6 o'clock in the evening.

13.12
1. True
2. True
3. False
4. False
5. True
6. True

13.13
1. I start work at noon.
2. I finish work at noon.
3. My brother starts work at noon.
4. My brother finishes work at noon.
5. They start work at noon.
6. They finish work at noon.
7. I start work at 2:30pm.
8. I finish work at 2:30pm.
9. My brother starts work at 2:30pm.
10. My brother finishes work at 2:30pm.
11. They start work at 2:30pm.
12. They finish work at 2:30pm.

14

14.3
1. We eat lunch at 3pm **on** the weekend / **at** the weekend.
2. She goes to bed at 1am **on** the weekend / **at** the weekend.
3. I go to work **from** Monday **to** Wednesday.
4. They eat dinner at 9pm **on** the weekend / **at** the weekend.
5. We finish work at 3pm **on** Fridays.
6. I eat breakfast at work **on** Mondays.

14.5
1. He **goes to the gym** on Tuesdays and Fridays.
2. They **go swimming** on Thursdays.
3. He **plays soccer** on Wednesdays.
4. I **take a bath** on the weekend.
5. You **read the newspaper** on Saturdays.

14.6
1. I watch TV **on** Sundays.
2. I take a bath **at** 7pm every day.
3. I go to bed **at** 10 o'clock **on** Sundays.
4. I get up **at** 8am **from** Monday to Friday.

14.10
1. True 2. True 3. False 4. True
5. False

14.11
1. I get up at 6am five days a week.
2. They go to bed at 11pm every day.
3. Sarah plays soccer twice a week.
4. Jamie washes his clothes once a week.

14.12
1. We get up **at** 7am five times a week
2. They go to work **from** Monday to Friday.
3. Linda washes her face **every** day.
4. Colin sleeps **from** 11pm **to** 6am.

15

15.4
1. She is not my sister.
2. That is not her car.
3. I am not 35 years old.
4. We are not Spanish.
5. Chad is not a vet.

15.5
1. He **is not** in the office.
2. She **is not** a businesswoman.
3. I **am not** 18 years old.
4. This **is not** a snake.
5. We **are not** artists.
6. You **are not** at work.
7. Dexter **is not** a cat.

15.6
A. 3
B. 1
C. 5
D. 2
E. 4

15.9
1. It **is not** 10 o'clock in the morning.
2. You **aren't** 35 years old.
3. I **am not** Australian.
4. My brother **isn't** married.
5. Tom and Angela **aren't** construction workers.

15.10
1. True
2. True
3. False
4. True
5. False
6. True
7. False

15.11
1. I am not at work.
2. I am not tired.
3. I am not 24 years old.
4. You aren't at work.
5. You aren't tired.
6. You aren't 24 years old.

7. He isn't at work.
8. He isn't tired.
9. He isn't 24 years old.
10. They aren't at work.
11. They aren't tired.
12. They aren't 24 years old.

16

16.4 🔊
1 I **do not** read the papers on Saturday.
2 The dog **does not** eat fish.
3 They **do not** go to the theater often.
4 Ben and I **do not** live on a farm now.
5 Theo **does not** cycle to work.
6 You **do not** work at Fabio's café.
7 Claire **does not** watch TV in the evening.
8 We **do not** play football at home.
9 Pierre **does not** wake up before noon.

16.5
1 False
2 True
3 False
4 False

16.8
1 We go to work every day. We do not go to work every day.
2 He watches TV in the evening. He doesn't watch TV in the evening.
3 You do not work in an office. You don't work in an office.
4 They play tennis. They do not play tennis.
5 She works with children. She doesn't work with children.

16.9 🔊
1 We don't work with animals.
2 I don't eat chocolate.
3 Sandy doesn't work in a hairdresser's.
4 Melanie and Cris don't have a car.
5 They don't live in Park Road now.
6 We don't watch Hollywood movies.
7 She doesn't drive a taxi.

16.10 🔊
1. I don't work outside.
2. I don't have a bicycle.
3. I don't play tennis.
4. You don't work outside.
5. You don't have a bicycle.
6. You don't play tennis.
7. We don't work outside.
8. We don't have a bicycle.
9. We don't play tennis.
10. Meg doesn't work outside.
11. Meg doesn't have a bicycle.
12. Meg doesn't play tennis.

16.11
1 Kim
2 Selma
3 Chiyo
4 Maria
5 Selma

17

17.4 🔊
1 Is Brad a nurse?
2 Are these my keys?
3 Are Ruby and Farid actors?
4 Is this his laptop?
5 Is Valeria his sister?

17.5
1 A
2 B
3 B
4 A
5 A
6 B

17.7 🔊
1 **Is** Holly your mother?
2 **Are** they from Argentina?
3 **Are** you a teacher?
4 **Is** this your dog?
5 **Is** there a post office?

17.11 🔊
1 **Do** you get up at 7am?
2 **Do** they live at number 59?
3 **Do** we finish work at 6pm today?
4 **Does** the parrot talk all day?
5 **Do** you work in a lab?

17.12 🔊
1 Do you live in New York?
2 Does she work on a farm?
3 Does he get up at 5am every day?
4 Do they come from Peru?
5 Does Brad work in the post office?

17.13 🔊
1 Do they live in New York City?
2 Does he work in a restaurant?
3 Does Lewis go swimming on Fridays?
4 Does Marisha work with animals?

17.14 🔊
1 **Does** she go swimming on Tuesdays?
2 **Do** you read the paper on Sundays?
3 **Does** she work with animals?
4 **Do** they work on a construction site?

18

18.3
1 True
2 False
3 False
4 True
5 False

18.4 🔊
1 No, it isn't.
2 Yes, it is.
3 Yes, she does.
4 No, I don't.
5 No, it isn't.

18.5 🔊
1 No, **I'm not**
2 Yes, **they do.**
3 No, **it isn't.**
4 Yes, **she does.**
5 No, **she isn't.**
6 Yes, **they do.**
7 No, **he isn't.**

19

19.3 🔊
1 What **are** their names?
2 What **is** the time?
3 What **are** my favorite colors?
4 What **is** the hotel next to?
5 What **are** they?
6 What **is** your uncle's name?
7 What **is** my name?

19.6 🔊
1 What is the time? It's 5 o'clock.
2 When is your birthday? July 23.
3 Which is your car? The red Ferrari.
4 Why are you here? For a meeting.
5 How old are you? I'm 25.
6 Who is there? It's me, Marcus.

19.7 🔊
1 **Where** are your parents from?
2 **How** old are you?
3 **When** is breakfast?
4 **Who** is your friend talking to?
5 **Why** is it cold in here?
6 **Which** person is your teacher?

19.11 🔊
1 When **does** she eat lunch?
2 Where **do** they live?
3 Which bag **do** you want?
4 Where **does** he come from?
5 When **does** the movie end?

19.12 🔊
1 Where does he play football?
2 When do you clean the car?
3 What time does the party start?
4 Which days do you play tennis?

19.13
1 When do you eat breakfast?
2 What do you study?
3 Where do you work?
4 Who is she?

19.14 🔊
1 **Where** do you work in the city?
2 **When** do you start work?
3 **What** time does it open?
4 **How** many people do you work with?
5 **Who** do you work with?

19.15
1 Her brother
2 Two
3 At 7am
4 Goes swimming
5 By the pool
6 Tomorrow

19.16 🔊
1. Where does Kate play golf?
2. Where do they play golf
3. Where do you play golf?
4. Where does Kate go to the gym?
5. Where do they go to the gym?
6. Where do you go to the gym?
7. When does Kate play golf?
8. When do they play golf?
9. When do you play golf?
10. When does Kate go to the gym?
11. When do they go to the gym?
12. When do you go to the gym?

19.17 🔊
1 How often **do** they play tennis?
2 Which office **does** he work in?
3 Where **is** the party?
4 What **do** you do?

19.18 🔊
1 What **is her cat called**?
2 Who **is your English teacher**?
3 Where **does Ben work**?
4 How **is your grandmother**?

21

21.3 🔊
1 **There are** two churches.
2 **There is** a swimming pool.
3 **There is** a library.
4 **There are** two castles.

21.4
1 airports
2 theaters
3 schools
4 hospitals
5 bars
6 churches
7 factories
8 offices

21.5 🔊
1 There are two schools.
2 There are two cafés.
3 There is a hospital.
4 There is a restaurant.
5 There are three stores.

21.7 🔊
1 There **isn't** a theater.
2 There **aren't** any factories.
3 There **isn't** a bus station.
4 There **aren't** any airports.
5 There **aren't** any churches.

21.10 🔊
1 There **are** no castles.
2 There **aren't** any factories.
3 There **are** no hospitals.
4 There **aren't** any churches.
5 There **are** no swimming pools.
6 There **are** no airports.

21.11
A 3
B 1
C 2
D 4

21.12
1 True
2 False
3 False
4 True

21.13 🔊
1 **There isn't** a park.
2 **There is** a hotel.
3 **There are** no cafés.
4 **There isn't** an airport.
5 **There are** two stores.
6 **There isn't** a train station.
7 **There are** two theaters.

22

22.3 🔊
1 **The** new teacher is called Miss Jones.
2 There is **a** good café in the park.
3 I work at **the** hotel next to the library.
4 There is **a** swimming pool near my office.
5 It is **the** dog's favorite toy.

6 Janie is **an** artist at the gallery.
7 See you at **the** café at the bus station.

22.6 🔊
1 There are **some** stores on Broad Street.
2 There is **a** café next to the castle.
3 There are **some** cakes on the table.
4 There is **a** phone here.
5 There are **some** factories downtown.

22.7 🔊
1 There **are** some supermarkets in town.
2 There **is** an office near the river.
3 There **are** some chocolate bars in my bag.
4 There **is** a hospital near the bus station.

22.10 🔊
1 Are there **any** stores on your street?
2 Is there **an** airport near Littleton?
3 Are there **any** mosques in the city?
4 Is there **a** swimming pool downtown?
5 Are there **any** offices in that building?

22.11 🔊
1 Is there a supermarket near here?
2 Are there any cafés on Elm Road?
3 Are there any hotels near your house?
4 Is there a café near your office?
5 Is there a bar next to the bank?

22.13 🔊
1 Yes, **there is**.
2 Yes, **there are**.
3 No, **there isn't**.
4 Yes, **there are**.
5 No, **there isn't**.
6 No, **there aren't**.

22.14 🔊
1 Yes, there are.
2 No, there isn't.
3 No, there aren't.
4 Yes, there is.

23

23.3 🔊
1 Wake up
2 Do
3 Start
4 Have
5 Wait
6 Stop
7 Work

23.5 🔊
1 Take the second right. The station is on the left.
2 Take the first left, then turn right. The restaurant is on the right.
3 Take the second left, and the hospital is on the right.

4 Take the first left, then go straight ahead. The hotel is on the right.
5 Take the first left, then turn left. The castle is on the right.

23.7 ◀))
1 The supermarket is **next to** the post office.
2 The museum is **behind** the café.
3 The station is **in front of** the church.
4 The cinema is on the **corner** of the intersection.
5 The post office is **between** the café and the supermarket.

23.10 ◀))
1 Don't read that book.
2 Don't go past the hotel.
3 Don't give that to the cat.
4 Don't have a shower.
5 Don't drive to the mall.

23.11
1 Library
2 Swimming pool
3 Movie theater
4 Science museum

24

24.3 ◀))
1 There are two hotels and three shops.
2 Hilda works in a school and a theater.
3 My uncle is a scientist and my aunt is a doctor.
4 Sue watches TV and she reads books.
5 The store opens at night and Jan starts work.

24.4
A 3
C 1
D 4
E 2

24.6 ◀))
1 There are hotels, bars, and stores.
2 Sam eats breakfast, lunch, and dinner.
3 I play tennis, soccer, and chess.
4 Teo plays with his car, train, and bus.
5 There is a pencil, a bag, and a cell phone.
6 My friends, girlfriend, and aunt are here.
7 Ling works on Monday, Thursday, and Friday.

24.8 ◀))
1 This is my car, but these aren't my car keys.
2 We eat a small breakfast, but we eat a big lunch.
3 I work from Monday to Friday, but not on the weekend.
4 The bathroom has a shower, but it doesn't have a bathtub.

24.9 ◀))
1 There isn't a bathtub, but there is a shower.
2 There isn't a bar, but there is a café.
3 The bag is Maya's, but that laptop isn't hers.
4 Si doesn't have any dogs, but he has two cats.
5 Sally reads books, but she never watches TV.

24.10 ◀))
1 Lu reads books **and** magazines.
2 I work every weekday, **but** not on weekends.
3 Jim is a husband **and** a father.
4 There is a cinema, **but** no theater.
5 There isn't a gym, **but** there is a pool.

24.11 ◀))
1 There is a cat and a rabbit, but there isn't a snake.
2 There is a doctor and a builder, but not a chef.
3 There is a laptop and a newspaper, but there isn't a cell phone.
4 There is a movie theater and a restaurant, but not a theater.

25

25.3 ◀))
1 He is a horrible man.
2 They are small children.
3 My uncle is a quiet man.
4 There is a large cake.
5 These are my old shoes.
6 There is a new supermarket.
7 You work in an old museum.

25.5
1. **small** 2. **beautiful** 3. **old** 4. **large** 5. **busy**
6. **horrible** 7. **beautiful**

25.6
1 The nurse is busy. She is busy.
2 The dog is quiet. He is quiet.
3 The patients are new. They are new.
4 The town is horrible. It is horrible.
5 The car is beautiful. It is beautiful.

25.8
1 beautiful
2 lake
3 large
4 mountains
5 restaurant
6 beach
7 busy
8 quiet

25.9 ◀))
1 **The** countryside **is** quiet **and the** trees **are** beautiful.
2 **The** city **is** horrible **and the** people **are** busy.
3 **The** hotel **is** new **and the** swimming pool **is** large.

4 **The** beach **is** big **and the** cafés **are** busy.
5 **The** city **is** old **and the** buildings **are** beautiful.

25.12
A 2
B 5
C 1
D 4
E 3
F 6

25.13 ◀))
1 There are **lots of** people.
2 There are **some** buildings.
3 There are **a few** cars.
4 There are **a few** parks.

25.14 ◀))
1 In the tree, there are a few birds and some apples.
2 In the sea, there are a few people and lots of fish.
3 In the countryside, there are some people and lots of trees.

26

26.3
1 lives there.
2 she's a farmer.
3 goes swimming.
4 it's new.
5 with people.
6 her aunt lives there.
7 lots of people.

26.4 ◀))
1 She lives on a farm because **she's a farmer**.
2 She works in a hotel because **she's a receptionist**.
3 They get up late because **they're students**.
4 We work with children because **we're teachers**.
5 You don't eat lunch because **you're busy**.
6 I work outside because **I'm a gardener**.
7 My parents go to the country because **it's quiet**.

28

28.3 ◀))
1 They **have** a car.
2 You **have** a chair.
3 He **has** a dog.
4 We **have** a daughter.
5 It **has** a door.

28.4
1 Maya **2** Ben **3** Ben **4** Ben

28.5
1. False
2. True
3. False
4. False
5. True
6. True

28.7 🔊
1. Kaleh does not have a dog.
2. You don't have a microwave.
3. Greendale does not have a church.
4. Alyssa and Logan don't have a garage.
5. We do not have a yard.

28.8 🔊
1. I have a couch.
2. I have some chairs.
3. I have a dining room.
4. We have a couch.
5. We have some chairs.
6. We have a dining room.
7. She has a couch.
8. She has some chairs.
9. She has a dining room.
10. She doesn't have a couch.
11. She doesn't have a dining room.

28.11
1. They have not got a couch. They haven't got a couch.
2. He has got three sisters. He's got three sisters.
3. You have not got a bike. You haven't got a bike.
4. We have got a microwave. We've got a microwave.
5. It has got a bathtub. It's got a bathtub.
6. They have got a cat. They've got a cat.

29

29.3 🔊
1. Do they have a toaster?
2. Do you have a new couch?
3. Does Ben have a washing machine?
4. Do we have an old armchair?
5. Does Karen have a large TV?
6. Does the kitchen have a sink?
7. Does the house have a yard?

29.4
1. Lucy
2. Lucy
3. Lucy
4. Tim
5. Tim

29.5 🔊
1. Do you have any chairs?
2. Do you have a kettle?
3. Do you have any plates?
4. Do they have any chairs?

5. Do they have a kettle?
6. Do they have any plates?
7. Does he have any chairs?
8. Does he have a kettle?
9. Does he have any plates?

29.7 🔊
1. No, I don't.
2. Yes, I do.
3. Yes, I do.
4. No, I don't.

29.8 🔊
1. No, he doesn't.
2. No, he doesn't.
3. Yes, he does.

29.10 🔊
1. Has this town got a theater?
2. Has your house got an attic?
3. Have they got laptops?
4. Has this coffee shop got a bathroom?
5. Have you got a cell phone?
6. Has the teacher got my book?

29.11 🔊
1. Yes, **she has**.
2. Yes, **it has**.
3. No, **they haven't**.
4. No, **it hasn't**.

31

31.3 🔊
1. Jake has **an** apple.
2. There is **some** coffee.
3. Reena eats **some** spaghetti.
4. There are **some** eggs.
5. I've got **some** bananas.

31.5
1. There is some milk. There isn't any milk.
2. Is there any chocolate? There isn't any chocolate.
3. Are there any apples? There are some apples.

31.6 🔊
1. Yes, **there is**.
2. No, **there aren't**.
3. No, **there isn't**.

31.9 🔊
1. There is **a bag of** flour.
2. There is **a cup of** coffee.
3. There is **a carton of** juice.
4. There are **two bowls of** spaghetti.
5. There are **two glasses of** milk.

31.12 🔊
1. **How many** glasses of juice are there?
2. **How much** water is there?
3. **How many** potatoes are there?
4. **How many** bars of chocolate are there?
5. **How much** pasta is there?
6. **How many** cartons of juice are there?
7. **How much** milk is there?

31.13
1. one bag
2. three
3. some
4. cheese

32

32.3 🔊
1. There **are enough** oranges.
2. You have **enough** pineapples.
3. There **are too many** apples.
4. You don't have **enough** bananas.

32.6
1. Too many
2. Not enough
3. Enough
4. Too much

32.7 🔊
1. There is **too much** sugar.
2. They **don't have** enough butter.
3. She has **too many** mangoes.
4. John has too many **eggs**.
5. There **aren't** enough oranges.
6. That is **too much** flour.
7. There **is** too much sugar in the cake.

34

34.2 🔊
1. Hannah **chooses** a yellow skirt.
2. Elliot and Ruby **buy** a new couch.
3. Sue **owns** an old winter coat.
4. Jess's dad **buys** her a new bike.
5. Chris and Lisa **own** a black sports car.
6. Gayle and Mike **sell** shoes at the market.
7. Mia **chooses** her red shoes.
8. The shoes **fit** me.
9. We **want** new white shirts.

34.3 🔊
1. They choose expensive blue sweaters.
2. Judith has some old brown hats.
3. This shop sells short red pants.
4. Tina owns cheap black shoes.
5. Jim buys a new black coat.

34.4

1. **new** 2. **cheap** 3. **white** 4. **long** 5. **black**
6. **black** 7. **old** 8. **new** 9. **expensive** 10. **cheap**
11. **red** 12. **long**

34.5

❶ a blue hat
❷ a new t-shirt
❸ a cheap skirt
❹ a black coat

34.7

❶ too cheap
❷ too expensive
❸ too long
❹ too short
❺ too old
❻ too new
❼ too big

34.8 ◀))

❶ Jim's pants are **too short**.
❷ Sam's dress is **too long**.
❸ Molly's sweater is **too small**.
❹ Helen's red hat is **too big**.
❺ Lili's shoes are **too big**.

34.9

❶ B
❷ A
❸ B
❹ A
❺ A

34.10 ◀))

1. These black pants are too big.
2. These black pants are big enough.
3. These black pants are too short.
4. My expensive pants are too big.
5. My expensive pants are big enough.
6. My expensive pants are too short.
7. My black dress is too big.
8. My black dress is big enough.
9. My black dress is too short.
10. My expensive dress is too big.
11. My expensive dress is big enough.
12. My expensive dress is too short.

35

35.4 ◀))

❶ This is a **horrible** old t-shirt.
❷ This is a **boring** movie.
❸ I have a **lovely** long dress.
❹ This is a **beautiful** bird.
❺ This is a **fun** party.

35.5 ◀))

❶ That is a horrible blue car.
❷ This is a fun short story.
❸ I have a lovely black cat.

---

❹ He has an ugly red house.
❺ They own a great new laptop.

35.6

❶ A
❷ B
❸ A
❹ A

35.8 ◀))

❶ Oh, no, the blue glass vase!
❷ We have two plastic chairs.
❸ What an interesting metal box!
❹ That's an expensive leather couch.

35.9 ◀))

❶ She owns some beautiful wooden chairs.
❷ We don't own those horrible
plastic plates.
❸ They have an ugly yellow car.
❹ He wears a boring blue sweater.
❺ She wants a new metal lamp.
❻ He owns a large fabric bag.
❼ Norah wants a new leather jacket.

37

37.3 ◀))

❶ We don't **go surfing** in the winter.
❷ Do you **go sailing** on the weekend?
❸ Tipo **goes cycling** five times a week.
❹ He **goes fishing** on the river.
❺ Sharon **goes dancing** with her friend.
❻ Do they **go running** every morning?
❼ He doesn't **go horse riding**.

37.4

❶ Wednesday
❷ Friday
❸ Tuesday
❹ Thursday

37.6 ◀))

GÉRONDIFS RÉGULIERS :
sailing, **snowboarding**, **skateboarding**
GÉRONDIFS AVEC DOUBLE CONSONNE :
swimming, **running**, **shopping**
GÉRONDIFS AVEC « E » TRONQUÉ :
skating, **horse riding**, **cycling**

37.9 ◀))

❶ Shala **doesn't play** tennis.
❷ Mina **plays** golf at the club.
❸ We **play** squash on Mondays.
❹ The dog **plays** with its ball.
❺ Maria **doesn't play** tennis.
❻ The kids **don't play** games at school.
❼ They **play** soccer at the park.

37.10 ◀))

❶ We **play** tennis every Tuesday night.
❷ They **don't play** golf during the week.
❸ You **don't play** volleyball at the beach.
❹ Do they **play** together every Saturday?

37.11

❶ Sara
❷ Chas
❸ Sara
❹ Cassie

37.12 ◀))

❶ Milo and I **go cycling** in the park
on Saturdays.
❷ The team **plays /play football** from 6pm
to 7pm on Wednesdays.
❸ Imelda **goes horse riding** once a month.
❹ Luther **goes fishing** during his vacation time.
❺ Hannah **plays tennis** with her cousin
on Monday evenings.

39

39.3 ◀))

❶ We never go to the mall.
❷ Sally and Ken usually cycle to work.
❸ My sister often works outside.

39.4

❶ usually
❷ never
❸ usually
❹ often
❺ always

39.5 ◀))

❶ Nico **usually** swims after work. He **never**
watches TV on the weekend.
❷ Meg **often** goes surfing in Hawaii. She
sometimes dances all night.
❸ Alma **always** reads on vacation. She
sometimes plays golf on Sundays.
❹ Carrie **usually** goes to bed late and she **never**
eats breakfast.

39.8 ◀))

❶ How often do they go to work?
❷ When do you get up?
❸ How often do you go on vacation?
❹ When do they go shopping?
❺ How often do you visit Mischa?

39.9 ◀))

❶ When do they visit their grandparents?
❷ When do we go skating?
❸ How often does he play hockey?
❹ When do you go shopping?
❺ How often do they see their parents?
❻ How often does he walk the dog?
❼ How often do we go skating on the lake?

179

39.10 🔊
1. When do you do yoga?
2. How often do you go to the movies?
3. How often do you go skateboarding?
4. When do you arrive at work?
5. How often do you go surfing?

40

40.3 🔊
1. Ava and Elsa love the mountains.
2. Shania hates mice.
3. Manuel likes his book.
4. Cats don't like the rain.

40.4
1. Imelda doesn't hate pasta.
2. My dog doesn't love steak.
3. Our grandfather doesn't like coffee.
4. I don't love the sea.
5. Sam and Jen don't hate hockey.
6. You don't like the countryside.
7. We don't like our new cell phones.

40.5
1. hockey
2. some actors
3. pizza
4. spiders

40.6 🔊
1. I love cats.
2. I love curry.
3. I love this house.
4. You love cats.
5. You love curry.
6. You love this house.
7. Milly hates cats.
8. Milly hates curry.
9. Milly hates this house.

40.9
1. D
2. B
3. C
4. A

40.10
1. True
2. False
3. False
4. True
5. False
6. True
7. False
8. True
9. True

40.14 🔊
1. Why does Una love skiing?
2. Why do they like this book?
3. Why doesn't Debbie like her job?
4. Do we like cooking?
5. Does she love surfing?
6. Do I hate working late?
7. Does Aziz love Ontario?

40.15 🔊
1. I like English class because it's interesting.
2. We love skating because it's exciting.
3. He hates cleaning because it's boring.

42

42.3
1. basketball
2. fish
3. Rome
4. gardener
5. Italian
6. running
7. cooking

42.4
1. A
2. B
3. A
4. C
5. A

42.5 🔊
1. Grace's favorite food is pizza.
2. Poppy's favorite sport is surfing.
3. Dylan's favorite animal is his horse.
4. Justin's favorite country is Australia.
5. Ling's favorite pastime is knitting.
6. Abdul's favorite color is purple.
7. Mira's favorite number is 10.
8. Jacob's favorite sweater is woolen.
9. Tori's favorite relative is her cousin.

42.6 🔊
1. Sam's **favorite band** is Big Bang.
2. Joe's favorite band is **Fun Sounds**.
3. Joni's **favorite restaurant** is Midnight Pizza.
4. Sam's favorite restaurant is **The Salad Bar**.
5. Joe's **favorite restaurant** is Burger Heaven.
6. Joni **loves the play** called Big Blue Sea.
7. Joe loves the movie called **Blue Soul**.

42.7
1. yoga
2. burgers
3. surfing
4. a restaurant

44

44.4 🔊
1. Paul cannot ride a bicycle.
2. Manuel cannot come to the party.
3. They can sleep in the tent tonight.
4. I cannot walk up the hill.
5. I can carry this box to the car.

44.5 🔊
1. Jo's pen doesn't work. She **can't** write her letter.
2. I understand the homework, so I **can** do it.
3. The museum is closed. We **can't** get in.
4. I have the car today, so I **can** drive you.
5. It's cold outside, so we **can't** have a picnic.
6. Tony needs to work late, so he **can't** come.
7. We **can't** play tennis. It's too dark.

44.6
1. Shirley can drive a car. Shirley can't drive a car.
2. Ben and Julie cannot carry boxes. Ben and Julie can't carry boxes.
3. Ilaria can spell English words. Ilaria cannot spell English words.
4. He can go to work. He can't go to work.

44.9 🔊
1. No, **he can't.**
2. Yes, **they can.**
3. No, **I can't.**
4. Yes, **I can.**
5. No, **we can't.**
6. Yes, **she can.**
7. No, **they can't.**

44.10 🔊
1. Can the dog jump over the wall?
2. Can Denise touch her toes?
3. Can I lift my son onto my shoulders?
4. Can Grandma see the TV?
5. Can I hit the tennis ball over the net?

44.11
1. True
2. False
3. True
4. True

44.12 🔊
1. Paul and Jerry don't like the ocean because they **cannot** swim.
2. I ride my bike to work because I **cannot** drive.
3. Jim cannot climb over the wall, but he **can** walk around it.
4. My mother **cannot** lift that bag because it's too heavy.
5. My sister Penny loves music and **can** dance to any song.

45.3 🔊
❶ Mary can speak French **excellently**.
❷ Roger can run very **quickly**.
❸ The old man walks **slowly**.
❹ He talks very **loudly**.
❺ She won the race **easily**.

45.5
RÉGULIERS
loudly, quickly, badly, easily
IRRÉGULIERS
fast, well, hard, early

45.6 🔊
❶ You speak English very **well**.
❷ Damian cooks burgers **badly**.
❸ I can get to your house **easily**.
❹ Benjy always listens **carefully**.
❺ My brother always works **hard**.
❻ Sammy always plays his guitar **loudly**.

45.10 🔊
❶ My horse is good at jumping.
❷ I am bad at getting up early.
❸ Mary is bad at writing German.
❹ Jo and Bob are good at swimming.
❺ Millie is bad at cleaning.

45.11 🔊
❶ Conchita is good at playing basketball.
❷ You can drive a van well.
❸ Shania and Dave are good at surfing.
❹ My father can't speak English well.
❺ Manu is bad at writing stories.

45.12
❶ Bad at
❷ Bad at
❸ Bad at
❹ Good at

45.13 🔊
1. I am good at cooking.
2. I am bad at cooking.
3. I am good at playing soccer.
4. I am bad at playing soccer.
5. I am good at history.
6. I am bad at history.
7. He is good at cooking.
8. He is bad at cooking.
9. He is good at playing soccer.
10. He is bad at playing soccer.
11. He is good at history.
12. He is bad at history.

46.3 🔊
❶ A tortoise walks very slowly.
❷ A chicken flies quite badly.
❸ Pigs eat very noisily.
❹ Monkeys climb trees really well.

46.5
❶ Really good
❷ Quite good
❸ Quite good
❹ Really good

47.4
❶ He wants to get a dog.
He would like to get a dog.
❷ You want to work in Turkey.
You'd like to work in Turkey.
❸ We would like to learn Chinese.
We'd like to learn Chinese.
❹ They want to start a rock band.
They would like to start a rock band.

47.5 🔊
❶ He'd like to act in a musical.
❷ He wants to be in the Olympics.
❸ He'd like to travel around Asia.
❹ She'd like to sail a boat.
❺ She wants to work with lions in Africa.

47.6 🔊
1. I'd like to climb this tree.
2. I'd like to climb that mountain.
3. I'd like to read a newspaper.
4. I'd like to read another book.
5. I want to climb this tree.
6. I want to climb that mountain.
7. I want to read a newspaper.
8. I want to read another book.
9. She wants to climb this tree.
10. She wants to climb that mountain.
11. She wants to read a newspaper.
12. She wants to read another book.

47.9
❶ He would not like to play tennis.
He wouldn't like to play tennis.
❷ She would not like to study science.
She doesn't want to study science.
❸ They would not like to go to work.
They wouldn't like to go to work.
❹ You wouldn't like to sing.
You don't want to sing.

❺ We would not like to go diving.
We don't want to go diving.

47.11
❶ No, she wouldn't.
❷ Yes, he does.
❸ Yes, he would.
❹ No, she doesn't.
❺ Yes, she would.

47.12 🔊
❶ He doesn't want to climb that hill.
❷ I wouldn't like to be a judge.
❸ They don't want to go to work today.
❹ She would like to play tennis tonight.
❺ I want to climb that tree.

48.5 🔊
❶ Jerry would really like to pass his driving test.
❷ Ben and Sam would really like to take an IELTS test.
❸ Helen would quite like to practice her English.
❹ I'd quite like to play the piano tonight.

48.6 🔊
1. I'd really like to practice my spelling.
2. I'd really like to do a biology degree.
3. I'd really like to learn English.
4. I'd quite like to practice my spelling.
5. I'd quite like to do a biology degree.
6. I'd quite like to learn English.
7. Laila would really like to pass her history exam.
8. Laila would really like to do a biology degree.
9. Laila would really like to learn English.
10. Laila would quite like to pass her history exam.
11. Laila would quite like to do a biology degree.
12. Laila would quite like to learn English.

48.9 🔊
❶ Emily has **a lovely home**.
❷ Sue always takes her lunch to **the office**.
❸ Can you see where **the church** is?
❹ Jim went to **bed** hours ago.
❺ Can you drive me into **town** later?
❻ I live next to **the university**.
❼ I leave **home** at 8am every weekday.

48.10
❶ Tom
❷ Frank
❸ Sophie
❹ Charlie
❺ Sarah

Index

Toutes les entrées sont indexées par
numéro de chapitre.
Les entrées principales sont en **caractères gras**.

182

Remerciements

Les éditeurs souhaitent remercier :
Jo Kent, Trish Burrow et Emma Watkins pour le texte supplémentaire ; Thomas Booth, Helen Fanthorpe, Helen Leech, Carrie Lewis et Vicky Richards pour leur assistance rédactionnelle ; Stephen Bere, Sarah Hilder, Amy Child, Fiona Macdonald et Simon Murrell pour le travail de conception supplémentaire ; Simon Mumford pour les cartes et drapeaux nationaux ; Peter Chrisp pour la vérification des faits ; Penny Hands, Amanda Learmonth et Carrie Lewis pour la relecture ; Elizabeth Wise pour l'indexation ; Tatiana Boyko, Rory Farrell, Clare Joyce et Viola Wang pour les illustrations complémentaires ;Liz Hammond pour le montage des scripts et la gestion des enregistrements audio ; Hannah Bowen et Scarlett O'Hara pour la compilation des scripts audio ; Heather Hughes, Tommy Callan, Tom Morse, Gillian Reid et Sonia Charbonnier pour leur soutien créatif et technique ; Vishal Bhatia, Kartik Gera, Sachin Gupta, Shipra Jain, Deepak Mittal, Nehal Verma, Roohi Rais, Jaileen Kaur, Anita Yadav, Manish Upreti, Nisha Shaw, Ankita Yadav et Priyanka Kharbanda pour leur aide technique.

Toutes les images sont la propriété de DK. Pour plus d'informations, rendez-vous sur **www.dkimages.com**.